SOCIAL MEDIA FOR WRITERS

Joanne Mallon

the big hand

Published by The Big Hand

First print edition 2015

A catalogue record for this book is available from the British Library.

www.joannemallon.com
www.twitter.com/joannemallon
www.bighandbooks.com

ISBN 978-0-9564163-8-4

CONTENTS

1. Introduction:
Why social media for writers?

The job of a writer is not just to write. It never has been. Writing is a calling, and most of us are called to it because we love it. We love to tell stories; both fiction and non-fiction. But being a writer involves more than simply putting the words down. Connecting with an audience, and marketing your work is your job as well. Charles Dickens, William Shakespeare, Oscar Wilde and Dylan Thomas are some of the many great writers who travelled far and wide to give talks and promote their work. What makes you think you don't have to do that too? It's not enough to just write it - you have to let people know that what you wrote exists.

Even if you are fortunate enough to be represented by a major publisher and have a publicist at your disposal around the time of your book launch, that doesn't mean they will do all the work for you. It's still down to you to bang your drum. Don't think that this means you have to be constantly hustling for sales and reminding the world of your own marvelousness. I find that a lot of writers who don't use social media imagine that this is what it's all about - a constant, draining round of selling and self-promotion. And this puts them off because let's face it, it sounds soul-suckingly unfun.

Think of social media as being more about human communication and hardly ever about selling, and you'll be on the right track. So it doesn't matter if you're not a good salesperson. All that matters is that you're willing and open to connect with and talk to strangers.

What can social media do for writers?

There are two main reasons why today's writers need to be interested in social media. First of all, it's an easy way to market both yourself as a writer (a brand, if the term doesn't make you heave) and your writing work (to bring readers to what you've created). It will both help you sell books and help you get a book deal in the first place. It will ensure that editors and publishers hear about you and mean that they are more likely to hire you.

These days, publishers and editors like a writer with a proven audience. The writer who is well established on social media is at an advantage to the one who is not. Of course, it doesn't mean that they're a better writer. But faced with two writers of comparable ability and experience, the one who's got thousands of Twitter followers is more likely to get the gig over the one who hasn't.

The second reason why professional writers and especially freelance journalists and copywriters need to pay attention to social media is because it can potentially be a source of income. A blog can act as a showcase for your writing and lead to you getting spotted for further writing work. Companies may pay you to post about them on your blog or theirs. And then there's social media management - writing blog posts and tweets; running Facebook pages etc. All of these are services that professional writers today get paid to do. And if you're experienced in these platforms, you could get paid to do it too.

Social media is as important for copywriters as it is for those with books to promote. As a copywriter, your name is probably not going on to the work that you do, but your reputation and personal brand still matter. People need to have heard about you and trust you if they're going to hire you. And how can they hear about you easily? I think you know where I'm going with this.

We're now at a point in time where pretty much every business will have a website, and very few people would start a new business without creating some sort of online presence. As the importance of social media has grown, businesses are expected to have some sort of social media presence as well. But many simply don't know where to go to get that, so they will look to anyone doing related work for them. If you're a freelance journalist or copywriter, social media could become a valuable arm of your writing business. If a company is hiring you to write their website copy or leaflets, they may also be interested in hiring you to write and manage their social media presence. These kinds of jobs will only continue to grow in the coming years, as other outlets for paid writing contract. This is one of the few expanding paid markets at a time when there aren't too many of those for writers. Social media skills are essential for the professional writer wanting to future-proof their business.

A note about how to use this book
Inevitably, this is a very information-dense book. Think of it like a fruitcake but with tips about Twitter rather than currants and raisins. This is information I've been building up over the last seven years. If you are brand new to social media and attempt to read the whole book in one go it might well blow your head off. I don't want that. Just like eating a whole Christmas cake - you could do it, but I wouldn't recommend it.

This introduction and the final resource chapter will apply no matter which social media platform you're using. Each of the other chapters focuses on a specific platform, so it's probably best to concentrate on the chapters that relate to the platform that interests you most, or whatever you're currently trying to get to grips with. And don't expect to get that grip overnight - give it at least a few weeks before you're familiar with the main features and ready to get to know another one.

It may be that you're already a Facebook user and you want to develop more there, or you registered a Twitter account two years ago and never used it but are ready to now. Pick the platform you like and go for it - Twitter is probably the best gateway drug since it's less time consuming and easy to pick up. You don't need to learn all the social media platforms in existence. I didn't learn this stuff all at once, and it would be unrealistic to expect you to either. I built up my knowledge over time and so will you.

If you get stuck with anything I am always happy to help if I can, so feel free to tweet me on @joannemallon or @SocMed4Writers or you can find more ways to get in touch on my website www.joannemallon.com

Social media is changing all the time. New platforms spring up, and old platforms fade or acquire new features. Think of it as a journey of learning, not just something you will learn once and be adept at. And the good news is that for the most part, it's easy to learn.

Your guide on this journey
I'm a writer just like you. A trained journalist, I've written two self-help books and contributed to a wide variety of publications, both online and offline. I'm also a career coach who specialises in working with media professionals, and sometimes I do social media consultancy for companies.

I've been coaching writers for over 13 years and am the UK's most experienced media career coach. I've worked with people all over the world, from writers just starting out and taking their first few steps in journalism, to writers who are very well established, widely published and at the top of their game. What I have to say to you in this book is both based on my own experience as a writer and sometime social media consultant, but also based on what I see happening with my clients who are writers.

My first love is writing and I often joke that I'm so addicted to it that I've got QWERTY imprinted on my fingertips (apologies for the lame writer joke). Frankly I don't know how I'd do this job without social media and the networks I belong to. I can directly trace back the majority of writing work I've done in the last five years to social media – either I saw an opportunity, or a made a contact or I heard about something that I wouldn't otherwise have known about, or somebody heard about me and approached me. For example, I heard via Twitter that my publisher was commissioning and ended up signing with them to write my first two books.

If you're not on social media, how many opportunities are you missing out on?

What difference does it make?
Social media helps sell my books. Every single time I mention my book about fear of driving on social media, at least one new person will pop up and say *I need that book*. And I know from tracking my links that many of them do go on to click through and buy a copy. For a self help book like that, with a very clear topic and title, social media works extremely well. People can tell instantly whether they need it or not.

For fiction writers it's a slightly different story, because you're not selling How To books. You're asking people to buy into your talent and creativity with both their money and their time. So for you, building the online presence for people to trust will take time and perseverance. It's unlikely to happen overnight, but that's OK because the audience that you build slowly from the ground up are more likely to stick with you.

There are many, many writers on social media, but there are many more readers (and of course the writers are readers too). So there we are, swapping book recommendations and discussing our latest reads. When I ask on Twitter for a new book recommendation for my book group, that's six copies sold right away.

Media in general has always been an industry that runs on contacts – people hire people they know, rather than going through the formal process of publishing a job ad and interviewing all candidates. And it's one of the most common things that new entrants to media will say – *how can I make the contacts I need?*

The great thing about the social media world now is that it's never been easier to connect with people. You tweet an editor, an agent or a publisher; have a conversation with them, and then when you pitch, they know your name. This is why it's important to use your own name on social media, or at least the name that you write under.

The other great thing about social media is that it is super easy to use. If it wasn't easy then it wouldn't have become so mainstream. You can be a technological ignoramus (I know I am) and you can still do it. If you know how to send an email, then you can use social media.

The only assets you need to get good at social media are ones that, as a writer, you've already got - namely curiosity and an open mind. So don't be scared. You've got this already.

And to look at it from another angle - why not social media? These tools are part of the trade right now. If you don't use them, or at least have a working knowledge of them, you risk getting left behind. Your peers are using it. The generation coming up behind you use it as naturally as breathing. Not using social media means you risk missing out on opportunities and all sorts of great stuff. You risk looking like a dinosaur.

Like a lot of writers, I am your classic introvert who likes nothing better than working from home, by myself and getting on with my writing. I will talk to real live people when pushed but it wouldn't be my preferred choice. And this is another big part of why I like social media. It's perfect for writers. It's perfect for introverts. You don't have to leave your house to do it, for a start. You don't need to find childcare and you can set your own hours. If you're up in the middle of the night, somebody somewhere on social media will be up too - often because it's not the middle of the night where they are. You don't have to attend any gawdawful networking events and stand there dry mouthed, wracking your brains for small talk and wondering how much is too much when it comes to the free bar.

Social media will bring you work, help you research and could even help you become a better writer. Isn't that worth ten minutes a day of your time?

How soon is now?

Your social media network, like any network, takes time to build. So although you can hop on this bus at any time, the earlier you start the better. Tomorrow isn't too late, but it's leaving it close to the wire. For example, if you are writing a book which isn't due to be published for at least a year, start building your social media presence now. Don't wait until publication day to enter the room with a great 'Ta daaaa!' It doesn't work like that. People need to get to know you before they will buy into you as a writer, even in cyberspace.

For some writers, social media can be the mother of all procrastination devices, and what people do when they haven't got much actual writing work on, but that doesn't mean there isn't treasure too. Remember that you don't need to be everywhere online all of the time (although if you want to look like you are, there's an app for that).

Pick and choose the social media platforms that appeal to you. Better to do one of them wholeheartedly than three of them half-baked. If you find you're spending more time on social media than actually writing, reel it back in a notch.

And of course, none of this means anything without the work. Being good at social media doesn't mean you're a good writer. Some aspects of social media, particularly blogging, will help to make you a better writer, but ultimately you still have to show up with the talent and the work. There's no app for that.

And neither does online entirely replace offline, real life marketing either. In fact it can connect to it incredibly well. The people who get to know you on social media could turn out to be the people who'll come to your talks or book launch. They may buy your books, hire you to work with them, refer you to others or get drunk with you in the pub. Every social media connection is a real person too, they're not just imaginary people who live on the internet. At least that's what they told me on Twitter.

How to find the time for social media?
We've all got the same 24 hours in a day, so it's not like you're trying to find some hidden jewel that nobody else has found.

What matters less than how much time you spend is how regularly you do it. So if five minutes a day is all you've got (and come on, we've all got five minutes), that's fine - as long as you keep using those five minutes, every day; or at least most days.

Yes, it will probably take you a bit longer than that at the start as you master the basics and put some effort into building your network. The more you do it, the easier it will become.

I personally dip in and out of social media depending on what else I've got going on. My iPhone is always with me so if I spot something that might make a good picture for sharing, either straight away or later, I can quickly snap one. Some days I don't use it at all, other days I'm on there yakking like a yak at a yakchat convention. Yes there's probably stuff I miss by not being on there more often but that's fine. I'm on there often enough to notice enough useful and important stuff.

The basics of social media
Use your own name on social media, or at least the name you write under. If you have a particularly common name and somebody's already registered it, play around until you find a

variation of it you can register. Maybe try firstname_lastname, or using your initials. If you have a particularly long name then you might need to shorten it a bit for Twitter. Twitter only gives you 15 characters to play around with for your username so use them wisely. Now you know how I ended up with the spectacularly ugly @SocMed4Writers

As a writer, your byline is your brand. What you want is for someone to see your name and think "he/she is really good at what they do" – and for them to know what you do; to know that you're a health journalist, or a romantic novelist or a business copywriter. Because if enough people know your name, what you do and how to get hold of you, they'll know where to come if they want to either hire you or recommend you. This is how you build the word of mouth that will support your business long term.

Keep your profile photo consistent across all social media and change it no more than two or three times a year. Try to keep it current to at least within the last decade so that people don't get too much of a shock when they meet you in person. A professional author's head shot is useful if you've got one, but a photo taken on a smartphone will do just as well. Hold your phone slightly above your head and look up into the camera for a natural facelift effect. This angle supposedly takes 10 years off you, which may or may not be a bonus depending on how much gravitas you want to project. Don't be shy of using your camera's inbuilt filters to look at your best. Aim for looking neither terrified nor terrifying. Show you, not your children or your dog. They're not the ones doing the writing.

Remember that as a writer, every single piece of writing with your name on it - whether it's a 140 character tweet or a 600 word blog post or a 90,000 word novel - is a published piece of work, and as such is representative of all your other published work. If you are annoying on Twitter then many people will assume you to be annoying in your other writing too.

You don't need to update your networks with your every move. Always think of it in terms of - Is this tweet/status update/blog post worth sharing? If another person was with me in the room now, would I tell them?

Always, with social media, give before you get. It's a two way street - a conversation, not a broadcast. You want more comments on your blog? Go and comment on other people's. You want more Twitter followers? Follow plenty of other people. Although we want to gain from social media, if you lead by taking then you won't receive much. Lead by giving and you will receive much more. As a writer, as in any profession, if you want to keep reaping a harvest then you have to keep sowing seeds. Don't go into social media with one hand out to take - go into it with both arms out to embrace and you will receive twice as much.

How to use social media effectively when you don't have much time
First of all, nobody expects you to use all of the social networks, all of the time. Those people you see who seem to be doing this probably either don't have much work on or are automating a lot of what you see, so when they post to one network their update automatically feeds out to others.

New platforms spring up all the time and it would be unrealistic to expect to use all of them effectively. But if you notice your friends start to talk about one particular platform or app or whatever, do hop in there and register under your me so at least you've claimed that little piece of online ate if it does turn out to be the next Twitter or Facebook. Always aim to be the first one with your name on any platform, wherever possible.

Social media is very much about you the person, so of course the more you do of it in person the better. But you can still automate some of it, and indeed you should. Posting in the middle of the night is a very effective way to catch potential readers in different time zones to you. Luckily you don't have to stay up until 3am to tweet at that time - there are tools to do that for you. The final chapter of this book is a resources section which will explain what you can use and how to use it.

Your social media plan

Until you get to the point where it's all fitting seamlessly into your life, you may find it more useful to have daily and weekly targets to stick to. If you're the kind of writer who can't work without a deadline then set yourself one - perhaps number of tweets each day or amount of time on social media.

It might surprise you to hear that I personally don't have a social media plan. When I am working as a social media consultant for others, we have a plan. For example, in my most recent role it was agreed that I would follow 30 new people on Twitter per day, post six new tweets per day, and post three to five updates per week to the Facebook page.

But for myself, when I'm not getting paid for this stuff, I mainly bumble along and do it by instinct. But I do bumble along every day. I'm on Twitter most days, though not so much at the weekend. I post to my blog once or twice a week depending on what I have to say.

Keep it clean

Be very aware that you're using social media for professional purposes. I don't post drunk, get into public fights or moan about my spouse (he follows me on Twitter, so I can't get away with it). I don't post anything too personal or embarrassing, so if things are going wrong in my life then I'll probably be at my least visual on social media. I'm not pretending that life is all ha ha ha, but just as it's not a good idea to let it all hang out in the workplace, neither does being active on social media mean you need to live your life in public. Not everything has to be shared.

The downside of social media AKA sucking up all your time and getting in the way of actual writing

One of the world's most well-regarded writers, Alan Moore, doesn't use social media and in fact doesn't even have the internet on in his house. That's how he's just finished a million word book. But he's Alan Moore and you and I are not. We still need our internets.

Like Bruce Springsteen who was Born to Run, you as a writer were Born to Procrastinate. It goes with the territory. Some of the worst procrastinators I know are also terrific writers who never miss a deadline. It's the dance we do. This is our dream job, and yet sometimes we want to put it off because a blank page is a scary thing. And rather than confront that, and test the limits of our ability to fill that blank page, we'd pretty much like to do anything else instead. Excuse me while I just share this cute picture of a kitten on Facebook.

I think that we often have an image in our heads that somewhere there's the uber-writer, the Ninja Freelancer, who jumps straight on to their keyboard first thing in the morning and doesn't stop until it's time for tea. They don't faff around on Twitter or Facebook, they don't play Candy Crush or World of Warcraft. Who is this mythical creature? If they exist they're very few and far between

If you are basically getting the work done that you need to do, and you're doing something to bring in new work; then you probably don't have as big a problem with procrastination as you think you do

The other way to look at the time you spend on social networks is that it's not wasting time at all – it's marketing your writing business and it's helping you get your next job. See it as a positive thing to do – making new connections that will lead to new ideas and new work. It can also be a stress reliever in between times when you're really concentrating hard. And anything which supports your sanity has to be a good thing.

My trick for avoiding wasting too much time on social media is my cup of tea rule. If I have a cuppa in front of me, then it's tea break time and I will check out what's going on on Twitter or Facebook. Other than that it's back to the keyboard.

And now - let's go tweet.

2. Twitter

Good for:

- Making connections with large numbers of new people
- Keeping tabs on breaking news stories
- Building relationships with editors and publishers before you pitch to them
- Hearing about unadvertised jobs

Not so good for:

- Fragile egos - the people you follow may not follow you, or they may unfollow you for no apparent reason
- The potential for time suckage is enormous
- For some people the fast flowing conversation is just too fast

I warn you now that this is by far the longest chapter in the book, so at this point you may wish to arm yourself with a beverage of your choice. Twitter has relevance for all types of writers, therefore there's a lot to say about it, for which I make no apologies. You might want to pack a snack too. Something oaty and not too high in sugar works well, I find. An oatcake or a handful of almonds, that sort of thing. Another warning - oatcakes aren't really cakes. Crushingly disappointing, I know

In this chapter we're looking at:

- What exactly is Twitter anyway? How can it help me as a writer?
- How to get started on Twitter
- Who to follow, how to attract followers and what to tweet about
- Tweeting professionally for clients - what's involved?

What is Twitter and why should I care?

Twitter is an online messaging service, where people publish and exchange messages of 140 characters or less. It has over 100 million users worldwide, but according to research published in 2014, around 44% of those accounts have never tweeted. Many come to tweet, and a fair few of those run away screaming because of all the noise. If you've registered a Twitter account but never used it, you're not alone.

Think of Twitter like a big pub full of Irish people, but with a higher proportion of sobriety (and by the way that isn't racist, as I am Irish and have been in a lot of pubs). Irish people tend to talk all at once, the conversation rolling like waves on the sea. If you were out with a bunch of Irish people there might be several conversations going on at once, with people dipping in and out of them, like dancing.

And Twitter's just like that - you don't have to wait for a natural dip in the conversation to have your say, because there isn't one. You just have to get stuck in. It's perfectly OK to join in a conversation that's already going on, even if you don't know the people involved. Dip in, dance a little, dip out. Don't expect to keep up with the conversations that went on when you weren't there. If it's important enough, you'll hear about it in due course.

Some people find the non-stop nature of Twitter very hard to handle, like exhausting yourself trying to keep up in a race that never pauses. If that's you then perhaps try following less people, or focus your efforts on a slower social media platform, like Google Plus. But before you retreat to the tumbleweed, think about what you'd be missing out on:

The benefits of using Twitter for writers:
- Showcase your skills - how well can you communicate in 140 characters?
- Use it to attract more work - it gives people a flavour of who you are and how you write.
- Social connections and a sense of buzz when you're working from home alone
- Use it like a search engine to help you find interviewees and case studies
- Meet new editors and publishers and find jobs. I've had masses of writing work that I can trace directly back to a single tweet or shout out from an editor. These days, many writing jobs only advertised on Twitter as the paid for journalism job ad market is disappearing
- Follow fellow journalists in your field for mutual support. Just don't moan about your editors because they're probably on there too.

One great aspect of Twitter is that it's very much about the here and now. If something's happening in the world, somebody somewhere will be tweeting about it, so it's very useful if you're a news reporter looking for up to date reactions. Just remember to verify them as you would any other source.

Social media as writers use it:

Ben Hatch @BenHatch
Ben Hatch is the best-selling author of the Radio 4 Book of the Year The P45 Diaries and a hugely popular tweeter with around 88,000 followers. Unsurprisingly, Twitter is his main social media focus: "I only really use Twitter. I think it works especially well for promoting ebooks that can be downloaded and read instantly. It's best not to overdo it, of course. Your Twitter feed shouldn't be a whole bunch of tweets about buying your book. Everyone gets bored of that quite quickly.

"I don't use a Twitter program or app. My following has been built up over about five years. As a writer I don't think I have gained any particular writing skills form Twitter apart from how to abbreviate and mangle words to fit the 140 character limit. If anything it's murdered my attention span. It does allow you great access to other writers, however. When you work from home as most of us do that's a reassuring community to tap into the thoughts of. It's basically my water cooler."

If you're looking to expand your network, then Twitter is the place to be. So how do you get yourself heard above that cacophony of voices? Well, one thing's for sure, it's not by shouting. It's by giving. Be generous with who you follow, who you retweet and who you talk to.

Social media as writers use it:

John Higgs @johnhiggs

Author John Higgs is best known for *The KLF: Chaos, Magic and the Band who Burned a Million Pounds* and *I Have America Surrounded: The Life of Timothy Leary*. He credits Twitter with helping him make the move to become a full time writer: "I wrote one book and was very unsure about it. I worried it was too strange and would condemn me to the lunatic fringe. So I just released it quietly as an independent ebook, to gauge what the reaction to it would be, and the only promotion I did was to tweet about it. As it turned out, the reaction to that book was fantastic, and a month or so later it had been picked up on by some influential people with credibility and a large audience. When that happened, suddenly doors opened with agents and publishers and book advances and foreign rights deals followed. Coming as someone who had no contacts in the industry, this was a godsend. I wouldn't have a career as an author if it wasn't for social media.

"I use Tweetdeck to manage Twitter, because it allows me to set up extra columns and filter all the various tweets however I need to. I have my regular column of everyone that I follow, plus a more select column of the people I know in real life or interact with most – all the people whose tweets I don't want to miss, basically. Plus you can keep a search running on subjects you may be researching in another column, which has proven itself invaluable in the past. You can also schedule tweets with software like this, although I've yet to use this myself.

John's advice to novice tweeters is to dive in: "The sooner you make the plunge, the more you'll benefit, so stop putting it off. I've developed a few personal rules over the years, but I wouldn't assume that they work for others. I'm wary of following back someone who follows over 5000 people, for example, as they are likely collecting numbers rather than engaging with people. I try to remember that my followers do not automatically share the same politics as me. I also don't use social media to criticise TV shows or other media that I've not enjoyed, especially if it is something that other people love. I think it's far better to just talk about things that are great. The pub is the correct place for slagging off films, or so it seems to me, but I know not everyone agrees."

Attracting Twitter followers

When actress Karen Gillan, AKA Amy Pond from Doctor Who, joined Twitter she amassed 45,000 followers in the first 15 minutes. I hope for her sake she had turned off email notification of new followers.

Alas for the rest of us, we're not Karen Gillan (which is a shame, because I'd love a go in the Tardis). It's not going to work like that for us. Unless you are a celebrity, people will not be queueing up to follow you without you showing willing by following at least a few of them back.

Occasionally authors who already have a decent sized audience will join Twitter, and this will lead to an immediate bump of followers, as their fans crowd round to hear what they've got to say. Meanwhile the humble author is panicking at their computer, wondering what's all this @ business, and just what is a retweet and a hashtag anyway? That's before they even start to craft a tweet that's both wise and amusing in 140 characters or less. Mustn't disappoint the readers.

What an awful lot of pressure. No wonder so many people abandon their Twitter accounts before they've even got started. There is no harm in building up your network slowly as you learn how to handle the platform. No followers? Don't worry about it. You're not ready for followers yet.

The basics - Getting started on Twitter

When you first go to Twitter.com it all looks very basic and plain before you sign up. It takes time to get Twitter working for you, so don't be put off if you find you just don't get what all the fuss is about at first.

When you first register and are creating your Twitter account, use the shortest version of your name that's available. As we know, your name is your brand as a writer, but if you have an especially long name then you will need to cut it down.

Your Twitter name, or handle, has to be no more than 15 characters in length. A tweet is only a maximum of 140 characters and when someone sends a tweet to you your name is included in that, so don't waste the space. You can change your Twitter name and keep the same followers, so all's not lost if you choose something then regret it.

You'll find the settings on the top bar of your Twitter page - it's on the top right hand side and looks like a little sun. That's where you go to change the look of your page and the words on your profile.

When you first create a Twitter profile, your profile picture will look like an egg. Change this straight away so people know it's you. It doesn't have to be your forever profile pic, just one to hold your spot for now. When you do get a head shot you're happy with, use the same one across all your social media platforms. It's only a very small picture, so it doesn't have to be magazine quality.

You will also need a header image - this is the horizontal picture that goes behind your profile pic. You can get a little bit more creative with this, and change it more often than you would your profile pic. I currently have an image of a close up of my book covers as my header. Yes it's a bit 'in your face' advertising wise, but then again it's only people who are taking a closer interest in you who'll go to your profile page and see this image, so for those people I think you can get away with advertising.

Twitter asks for a location and you can be as specific or vague about this as you want. You can always put Worldwide if you're an international kind of person. I put my real town, Brighton, because I am interested in connecting with local people, plus even people who aren't from Brighton often like it, so it all adds to the warm and fuzzy feelings and you can never have too many of those.

Include a link to your website or blog, depending on which is most important to you to promote. If you don't have either of those yet, you could link to your Amazon author page, or a specific book page if that's what you're promoting at the moment.

The space for your biography is very small, only 160 characters, so choose wisely what to add in and leave out. It's a good idea to refresh this section occasionally - perhaps by showcasing new work, recent achievements, changing background images, adding new images etc. Don't change it too often as you'll confuse people but update once or twice a year as appropriate. If you say you're a journalist then this will help you attract followers, especially PRs in your field. Writer is probably a bit too vague to do that. If writing is not your day job, but that's how you want to promote yourself, go right ahead. Take some time to tweak this page. Until you have some followers hardly anybody's going to see it anyway so make the most of your privacy.

You can also customise the whole background of your Twitter page, either using a number of pre-made templates or by uploading your own image. Many brands use this space for a bit of extra advertising, and if you don't have your book covers in your header they could go in the main background instead.

If you have a smartphone (and if not, why don't you? Twelve year olds have smartphones these days and they're probably not presenting themselves as a professional writer), upload the Twitter app to help you check in and send tweets when you're out and about.

You can also manage your Twitter account via systems such as Hootsuite or Tweetdeck, but if you're just getting started you don't need to think about them just yet. More about them in the last chapter on social media tools and resources.

Should your Twitter account be private?
You'll see that some accounts have a little padlock next to the user's name, and don't let you see their tweets unless the account holder has given permission - these are private

accounts. Since you're essentially there to publicise your writing, a locked down private account would be pointless to you. I've known journalists temporarily make their accounts private when they have written something controversial and are copping a lot of online abuse for it, so if you write that kind of stuff then this may be something to consider in the future.

A private account is useful for the very young and those in sensitive occupations. Some very high profile celebrity tweeters also have private accounts where they can banter with their mates, unseen by the vast majority. But social media, by its very nature, is not private and it's very hard to make it so.

If you are nervous about using social media then you might consider starting with a private account so less people will see if you goof up. It's the equivalent of dipping a toe in the water. Though really, if you want to make it work for you then you have to dive right in.

Twitter basics - Sending tweets
A tweet is a message of 140 characters or less, sent out via the Twitter network. If you want your tweet to be a call to action, think of it like a headline and write accordingly. Don't tweet just for the sake of it, though neither does every tweet have to have the wisdom of Rumi.

The *Compose New Tweet* section is on the Home screen, top right hand side next to your profile pic. Simply type what you want to say into this box, click *Tweet*, and it's published.

Twitter has an automatic link-shortening tool, and if you include links then they will be shortened. The site counts the number of characters as you type them, so it's easy to see if you've gone over 140 characters and cut back if necessary. You don't have to fill up the full 140 characters - it is best practice to make original tweets shorter. This gives users who wish to retweet/republish the option to add their own comment at the start.

If you tweet anything then it has the potential to be seen by everyone who is following you, if they happen to be online at that time. If you haven't got many followers, and they're not online anyway, not many people will see your tweets. The more followers you gain, the more people will see your tweets.

In reality only a small proportion of your network/followers will be online at any one time. Therefore if you have a message which you want as many people as possible to see (eg a link to your latest blog post or news of your new book), it's advisable to tweet it more than once. If you're sending the same tweet multiple times, leave at least a three hour gap and tweak the words so not every message is exactly the same. Scheduling tweets for the middle of the night will catch people on opposite time zones.

When you log in, you don't have to scroll back to catch up on all the tweets you've missed - there are simply too many to do this. Scroll down a little if you want to, but generally it's fine to just jump into the conversation then and there.

Use a conversational but business-like tone - social media is a relaxed, less formal type of communication. Be cautious with jokes as not everyone shares the same sense of humour and it's easy to offend. Of course you can be funny, and it's probably better if you are, but just like real life, not everybody will get your sense of humour.

Absolutely never use offensive language or any information which may be defamatory or damaging to your clients. If you're tweeting on behalf of a client, every tweet reflects on the company as a whole. If you're angry with someone, don't take it to Twitter as it will reflect badly on both of you.

Historically Twitter has had a reputation for being a place where people share pictures of what they had for breakfast, but really it's what you the user make of it. If you want to share pictures of your breakfast with your friends then that's fine, but if you want to use it in a more formal, business-like way then that's fine too.

@ messages and replying to tweets

A tweet which is preceded with the @ sign goes to the username you've addressed it to only. But it is not a private message - it can be seen by anyone who follows both you and the person you're tweeting, plus anyone who looks at your profile page. Think of it like a postcard which is sent from one person to another but which can potentially be read by anyone.

If you have any other characters at the start of your message then it will be published to all of your followers.

So sending:

@joannemallon Hello!

would only be seen by me, plus anyone who follows both you and me, whereas sending

Hello @joannemallon

will be seen by all of your followers, plus me even if I don't follow you. It can be a bit irritating for anyone for whom the message isn't relevant so do it sparingly.

When you include another user's name in the body of the message in this way, it's known as tagging, and you would do this if you wanted to attract someone else's attention.

You can send an @ message to any other Twitter user that you want to get in touch with, which makes it great when you're researching and looking for case studies.

It's polite to reply to anyone who tweets @ you. If you're using the Twitter app on your phone, it will tell you when you've received an @ message. Immediacy is very important on Twitter, since it's such a fast running stream. Reply to messages days or even weeks later and you might as well not bother as the conversation has moved on so much. So for example if you're searching for people tweeting about a particular topic, keep an eye on when they were doing it as much as what they were saying. If it was days ago, they've probably left the building already.

Aim to respond to @ messages within 24 hours (the Reply option will appear when you hover over the message). It's a good idea to check your Twitter account at least twice a day for @ mentions, replies to questions etc.

Click on the *Notifications* column (on the top of the main home page) to see all interactions and messages addressed @ you. This column will also show you if there's any other activity on your account, such as new followers. You'll see a little number appear above the word Notifications when you log in indicating how many new interactions you've got.

Direct messages

If you want to send a message that's more private than an @ message, Twitter has a direct messaging facility. This will only be seen by the sender and receiver, though there's nothing to stop the receiver from taking a screenshot or telling other people about the message. If an @ message is like a postcard then a DM is like sending a letter. You can't DM just anybody - they have to be following you.

Retweeting

Retweeting or RTing refers to re-publishing someone else's original tweet to your network. You would do this if you think a particular tweet is of interest to your network. Simply hover over any tweet and the Retweet option will appear, still credited to the original writer.

If you want to engage with another user (especially if they're not following you and you want them to notice you) then retweeting their tweets can be a good way to do it. So you might retweet stuff from an editor or agent you're aiming to get to know.

Including a few retweets amongst your original tweets is good practice, and particularly useful when you don't have much new to say yourself. If you like it and think your network will like it too, RT it.

I tend to RT opportunities - job ads, blogger shout outs and anything I think is worth passing on. I hope this makes people feel it's worthwhile following me and makes up for the times I'm plugging my books and blog posts.

Following new people and attracting new followers

Who to follow

- People you've worked with in the past
- People you'd like to hire you
- Staff from publications you want to be featured in – and look to see who they follow
- Other writers in your sector
- PRs in your sector
- Relevant news outlets for your sector – especially overseas outlets
- @IPCJobs @MediawomenUK both regularly tweet writers' job news
- Sparky and interesting people. How interesting you find Twitter to be is largely determined by who you're following. If it's not lighting your fire, unfollow the dullards and find somebody more interesting to follow.

Following other people, preferably new people you haven't been in contact with before, is at the heart of using Twitter and is the best way to expand your network and encourage new people to follow you.

You can follow any one at all on Twitter regardless of whether you already know them. In this respect it's different to Facebook or LinkedIn where you probably only connect with people you already know.

Because the point of connection is looser on Twit
of disconnection is looser too, and you can unfr

you choose to (and be unfollowed) without it being too big a deal. There are programs you can use to monitor who has unfollowed you but this is of limited use. What matters more is that your network as a whole is growing.

When you're starting out, be generous with who you follow. Follow anyone who seems like a good egg. Around one in three will follow you back, possibly more once you start to build up a bigger community.

Don't feel that you have to stick to engaging with writing-related people, even though ultimately you are there to promote your writing career. Follow any account that seems interesting. Follow your passions, because the people running these accounts are people with passions that match yours.

Follow celebrities if you really are a fan, but truth be told, many of them are quite dull on Twitter. Plus, as a writer their poor grammar and use of text speak will probably tick you off. Personally I avoid celebrities on Twitter, and also people who think they are celebrities on Twitter.

I don't automatically follow everybody back, but I follow back anyone I've met personally, anyone who lives in the same town as me and anyone I've talked to (on Twitter).

Following in the Twitter sense means subscribing to someone's updates. You can do this by clicking the '*Follow*' button on that person/business's Twitter profile page. When you're following someone you will then see all of their updates on your homepage if they tweet whilst you're on Twitter.

There are a number of different ways to find new people to follow on Twitter.

The simplest way is to use Twitter's own recommendation tool, which can be found by clicking on *View All* in the *Who to Follow* section on your home page. They move it around the page from time to time - currently it's on the top right hand side. This tool looks at who you already follow and who those people follow, and produces a list of recommendations based on that.

The *Who to Follow* tool can be useful, but it's not very sophisticated. It will recommend a lot of celebrity accounts, because a lot of people follow celebrities.

When you are on another user's profile page and click the Follow button, Twitter then refreshes the page and usually (not always) suggests two other accounts you might like to follow. This is based on an analysis of the person you've just followed, and who you already follow - it's looking for common ground between you both. Sometimes these suggestions are useful and you will have found a couple more people to follow. If they're not, just ignore.

Another way to find new people to follow is to look at organisations relevant to your writing niche and see who's following them and might be appropriate for you to follow too. Or you could use the search facility to search for particular job titles or industries - use this to look for editors and publishers.

You can look at any Twitter account and click the *Followers* or *Following* tab to see who's following them, and who they're following, and the account holder will not know that you've done this. So do look at other people's accounts - perhaps colleagues and other writers in your field - and see who's in their network, and perhaps follow some of those people too.

When you're looking at anybody's list of followers or people they're following, the list is in chronological order. The people at the top are the most recent contacts, and the ones at the bottom are the most long-standing contacts, since that's who they followed or were followed by first. So if you're researching someone you'd like to work with, scroll down to the bottom of their lists and you'll see who their pals are. Because they probably started their Twitter network like most of us do - by following their friends and having their friends follow them back. Yes we're getting into borderline stalkery behaviour by noting things like this, but the media and the literary world can be close knit communities and it can be helpful to know where the lines cross.

When you follow someone new, they will probably get an email to alert them to this fact (you can change this in the Email Alert settings but most people don't bother). The email will contain the text of your Twitter biography, and this is why it's so important - it will be seen by most of the people you follow, regardless of whether they follow you back or visit your profile page. Even if you never actually speak on Twitter and they don't follow you back, this is a small chance to get noticed and make someone new (perhaps an editor or a publisher) aware of your name. Those 160 characters that you fill with your profile are deceptively important, since they are a mini advert that will be winging its way to anyone you choose to follow.

You'll also get an email when somebody new follows you (unless you've disabled that setting) so you can decide whether you want to follow them back or not. You don't have to, but when your network is getting going you might as well.

If you have a particular niche that you write about, follow people associated with that niche. Follow any editors or publishers you want to get noticed by. Jobs for writers are rarely advertised and are much more likely to be advertised via personal contacts and word of mouth. Follow anyone you'd like to hire you. Of course, there's no guarantee that they ever will hire you, but at least you're increasing your chances.

You don't have to research the people you follow in depth - simply take a quick glance at their profile to see if they might be someone you'd like to connect with, and if they are actively using Twitter now (no point in following an abandoned account). Since this is a pretty fast process, you can follow 100 new people a week quite easily, more if you have the time or inclination. When I'm focusing on establishing a new Twitter feed I tend to follow 30 new people a day, which takes less than 10 minutes.

It's a good idea to actively follow plenty of new people until you get your own follower numbers up to at least 1000. At that point you can ease off (or carry on if you're going for bigger numbers). When you are building your community and focusing on your follower numbers, set a target for the number of new people you are going to follow every day or week.

It may seem like an enormous effort to follow hundreds of people, but it's not like you have to keep tabs on them all like some errant teenage offspring. Only a small proportion will be online at the same time as you. Some of them may tweet very little, or not at all. It's easier than you think to follow a large number of people at once, but if it starts to feel like too much then unfollow those who interest you least.

How many people can you follow?

You may find that you hit a follower limit. Twitter will let you follow as many people as you like, up until you're following 2,001 people. At that point, you can only follow 10% more people than follow you, so if you're following the maximum 2,001 people, you need to have at least 1,850 following you before they system will let you follow any more. The point of this is to encourage interaction and discourage accounts that are following masses of people but not attracting any followers themselves.

If you hit that 2,001 limit but want to keep growing your network, you will need to unfollow some people before you can follow anyone new. Use a cleanup tool to examine your account and decide who to unfollow - probably accounts which have stopped tweeting, or people who aren't following you back. The cleanup tool ManageFlitter is great for this - more of that in the resources section.

Social media as writers use it:

Jason Arnopp @jasonarnopp

Author and screenwriter Jason Arnopp has got the highest Klout score of anyone I know, which in social media terms means he's very well-connected. With over 16,000 followers, it's not surprising that Twitter is a priority for Jason: "Twitter's definitely my first and main port of call when it comes to social media, because it can allow you to reach many people instantly. I also have one of those 'official' Facebook pages and a Google+ profile, which I've twinned with my blog.

"I've run a Blogspot blog since 2007. Whenever I make a new post on there, I tell people about it a few times over the next few days, via Twitter, Facebook and Google+. Best to focus on one or two platforms. Three at the most.

"Interacting with 16,000 followers doesn't present as much of a challenge as you might think. It would be far more of a challenge to try and follow 16,000 people! It's estimated that, on average, about 5% of your followers see any one of your tweets, so it's not as if you have the attention of anything like all of them at any one time. Having said that, it is often hard or even impossible to reply to everyone who tweets at you. Sometimes you have to reply to all your followers as one, especially if many people are asking the same question.

"My follower count has grown naturally since 2009. I think it's relatively high because I've operated in quite a few different fields in my career. I started out as a rock journalist, then moved into writing for Heat magazine and also Doctor Who Magazine. So there are three different areas which people might know me for, or be interested in. Then when you factor in the fiction-writing – which again includes Doctor Who work and a horror film called Stormhouse – that potentially brings more people to your door.

"I've made contact with a lot of people who have become acquaintances or even friends, even though I've never actually met them. Generally, I'll then befriend them on Facebook, a platform which tends to make it easier to get to know people better. Social media has become such an integral part of most of our working lives that it can be hard to pin down where opportunities sprang from. I'd imagine that my reasonably prominent Twitter profile might have influenced my literary agent's decision to take me on. It might also have led producers or editors to take me more seriously. Perception is vitally important these days, provided of course that you can back it up with the work.

"I've also gained a bigger audience. I can tell people when I've written something new and where they can find it, which is invaluable in these days when we writers often feel adrift on a sea of signal-noise, trying to get noticed. In terms of any skills gained, Twitter's restrictive character count has probably helped me keep my writing quite sparse and economical. It has also taught me to exercise restraint when marketing myself."

Jason's advice to new tweeters is to have fun "Don't expect your profile to grow quickly, unless you find yourself at the epicentre of some major international scandal, or live-tweeting from a site where aliens have landed. Follow people you're genuinely interested in. Don't do favours for people (e.g. RT-ing a tweet about their new novel) purely because you're expecting them to reciprocate – it probably won't and indeed shouldn't work like that. Never badger people to follow you back or ask why they've unfollowed you. Just be nice, be genuine and try to strike the right balance between plying your own wares, talking about everyday stuff, putting the world to rights and simply engaging with others. People tend to unfollow pretty quickly if you just post the same 'Buy my book!' tweet every day. Put info about your book somewhere in your Twitter bio – you can insert links into it. If someone organically comes to like you as an online presence, they'll be more likely to check out your writing. Not that there's anything at all wrong with directly pushing your writing from time to time – it's just all a matter of degree."

A quick way for bloggers to build up followers
One fast way to build up your Twitter followers is to run a giveaway on your blog and ask people to follow you as one of the entry requirements. I did this recently and packed on around 150 new followers very quickly. The downside of doing this is that those people aren't following because they're interested in your work - they're following because they wanted to enter a contest. Of course, you can always convert those people to readers, and the extra bump in follower numbers will help you appear more popular to potential clients and editors.

When to follow back
Following back refers to following another account which has recently started following you on Twitter. In general it is considered good etiquette to follow back people who follow you, but it's not compulsory. You're here to meet new people, so be generous in following back.

To follow back, from the home page click on the Followers tab and this will give you a list of all your followers, with most recent listed at the top. Click on the Follow tab for those you wish to engage with.

Spam and false accounts

There are many spam and false accounts on Twitter, and from time to time they will start following you. For these accounts it's a numbers game - they're automatically following large amounts of people in order to build up their own followers so that the account can later be sold on.

Spam accounts are quite easy to spot as they simply don't look like anything a human being would produce. The clues are:

- No profile image
- No biography
- No tweets
- Following a very large amount of people (probably done automatically)

Some spam accounts are of a sexual nature and will carry X-rated profile pics. These need to be blocked because it looks unprofessional to have accounts like this in your follower feed. Once you block a user on Twitter they will not appear in your follower list and will not be able to tweet to you. To block, go to their profile page and hover over the small head and shoulders icon (next to the *Follow* button) and a list of options, including *Block*, will appear.

Other spam accounts you can leave alone - they will unfollow eventually when you don't follow them back.

Sometimes spam accounts will send links containing viruses - do not click on these. Be cautious if someone you don't know sends you a link.

Blocking people on Twitter

Hopefully you won't have to do this very often, but as previously mentioned, Twitter gives you the option to block someone if for whatever reason you don't want to interact with them. You can also report them to Twitter HQ if you believe a tweeter has been unlawful, overly offensive or spammy in some way.

All you have to do is go to that person's profile and hover over the circle next to the button that says Follow or Following. This will bring up a number of other options, and block and report are both in there as options to click.

Once you have blocked someone, you won't be able to see their tweets and they won't be able to follow you. However, they will still be able to see your tweets if they're determined to by going directly to your profile page. They won't be able to follow you and your tweets won't show up in their regular twitter stream, but it doesn't mean that you've hidden from them altogether.

Use the blocking function sparingly, if at all. Sometimes blocking people can inflame them and make the situation worse. If you write particularly controversial stuff then you may come in for some online flak from time to time but like all storms it will blow over. You could drive yourself mad if you start blocking everyone who disagrees with you on social media.

Organising your network by creating lists

If you find yourself following a large volume of people, organising them via a list can be a good use of your time so that you can see tweets from smaller groups of people at once, and don't miss their tweets. The list function helps you to follow larger numbers of people and also streamline what you see.

When you add someone to a list, they will get a notification that you've done so, and again this can serve to attract their attention and remind them that you exist. I've just been added to a list called *Awesome Journalists We Would Like to Work With* and this both attracted and repelled me, so I clicked on the tweeter it came from, who turned out to be a PR company. So when you're naming your lists, be aware that these names are publicly visible, and calling a list *Editors I Plan to Stalk* or *Writers I Plan to Murder So I Can Have Their Book Deal* etc won't do you any favours in the long run.

Depending on how you use Twitter, you may find it useful to separate people out into

- Close friends & family
- Editors
- Publishing contacts
- Clients (past & future)
- Media relevant to your writing niche

Personally, even though I've been using Twitter since 2008, I've still not got round to dividing people into lists. Possibly I am just lazy and am seriously missing a trick here. I prefer to keep on top of who I'm following simply by following less people. The downside to doing it like this is that it does somewhat limit the growth on your own account. Until I get that job as a companion on Doctor Who, I'm not going to attract 100,000 followers while I'm only following about 700.

Dude, why did you unfollow me? Was it something I tweeted?

Your follower numbers will go up and down over time. Don't bother to track who's unfollowed you. There are a number of programs that will do this for you (and I did use one for a while) but honestly, it will drive you mad and do nothing for your self esteem. People follow and unfollow each other for all sorts of reasons, and they're very unlikely to be personal. Sometimes Twitter itself gets a bit glitchy and will unfollow people without you even realising it.

Many users with large followings get like that because they use an automated program to grow their accounts. How this works is that it follows the maximum number of people allowed per day, then after a few days it unfollows those who didn't follow back. So if you don't follow them back quickly enough, they and their bot will be gone. This is why you might find your follower numbers fluctuating, as some accounts will unfollow you if you don't follow them back quickly.

Down with automation

Don't use auto replies. People hate them. Typically, an auto reply is when you follow someone and get an automated message back saying *Hey, thanks for following. Check out my website on www.blahdeblahdeblah.com* By all means do thank people for following you, but do it in a personal and sincere way with a tweet you just wrote and not one you cut and pasted to 100 people. (Most people don't thank new followers, it's not really required).

What to tweet about

This is the biggest sticking point for many people getting started on Twitter - what do I tweet about? How do I know it's interesting? The official term for it is 'engaging content'. Be engaging and you will engage people. But how do you know what's engaging and what's dull as dirt?

Well, the truth is that you don't. This is my rule of thumb - if I would want to tell somebody else about it, then I'll tweet about it. If an article or a thought or a picture is good enough (in my opinion) to share, then I'll share it. I accept that not everybody will find the same things interesting that I do. Sometimes I tweet something I felt sure was likely to get a big response and it sinks like a stone in a still lake.

Stick with tweeting the three Cs and you won't go wrong
- Created - Original tweets and links to material created by you. Fresh stuff from your own head.
- Curated - Links to material not written by you, but which you thought was worth sharing. If the original creator is on Twitter, then you can tag them by including their @ username and possibly make a new connection with them.
- Conversation - Chatting, basically. Never discount the power of small moments, they're what the world turns on.

Always write with the reader in mind. It's not the place to broadcast your own personal stream of consciousness. Save that for your blog. Write like a human being and people will connect with you as one.

This is the sort of stuff I've been tweeting about lately:
- Links to jobs I thought sounded cool, that somebody in my network might want to apply for. Obviously I don't link to jobs I'm planning to apply for myself. No point in needlessly attracting competition.
- Links to articles and blog posts I had read and thought were good

- Links to writing I've had published. I include the publisher's @username so they can see I've tweeted.
- A picture of a birthday cake I made and was proud of. Hey, that Minecraft cake took me all afternoon.
- A lame joke I stole off Tumblr about a film I went to see.

Probably the number one thing I get a reaction to is if I ever post a picture or story about my cat. I have an enormous, bad tempered cat who sometimes stands like a man and poses for pictures. Cats are incredibly popular on social media, so if you have one then you're in the game already.

As a writer, you are at an advantage when it comes to a lot of social media, since words are your thing. So don't worry too much about what you'll tweet about. The words will come. Not every tweet has to be earth-shatteringly devastating in its wisdom. But don't use text speak and stick to accurate spelling and grammar as much as possible. Occasionally you may have to commit a grammar crime in order to fit into the 140 character limit, and it will cause you physical pain to do so, but such is the lot of the tweeting writer.

A tweet with your name on it is still a piece of published writing with your byline on it, so treat it accordingly. By all means have a private account with which to shoot the shit with your friends. Ultimately, you are showing up in a professional capacity, and displaying what you have to offer as a writing professional. So be professional about it.

Ask questions, especially when they relate to your writing. Maybe you're doing some research or looking for a case study. Post about your life - at least the aspects you're happy to share.

None of this is private and it can all be found by Google. Yes you can delete tweets but you can't reclaim the eyeballs that might have seen your tweet when it was first published. Before you tweet, think about how much of yourself you want to give away. Are you happy to include pictures of your family? Do you need to get the cat to sign a release form?

Don't post drunk, and avoid getting into the habit of posting tipsy. Seriously, just make it a rule. You'll thank me eventually. Also, don't be a dick. I probably should have put that right at the top of the chapter and saved myself 10,000 words. Don't be a dick on Twitter. That's the main thing you need to know.

Don't whine about not having enough writing work, or moan about having too much. Both are off-putting. One writer I know has a habit of complaining that he's struggling to hit his deadlines, which could be seen as charmingly self-deprecating, though equally it's not going to endear you to somebody who wants to hire a writer who can hit their deadlines. More than one editor has told me that they are put off hiring writers who talk on social media about how busy they are. In the editor's mind, this translates that you're not available for more work, or you might not give it your full attention.

Don't harass people to buy your book. You can get away with an occasional "Great news, my book about fly fishing is back in stock at Amazon" but don't over do it. If you refer to it, always include the subject of your book so somebody looking for information about that topic can find you more easily. Aim for no more than 1 in 15 tweets to be promotional.

If you post something that's likely to draw a response, stick around to see who responds and reply to them quickly. But think long and hard before getting into arguments online, especially if they're directed at somebody in particular.

If you have strong opinions on religion and politics, think carefully about whether you want to express them on social media, especially if they don't relate to your writing. You may draw some like-minded followers, but equally you may turn some off. But then again, you don't want to be the blandest of the bland either. Your social media is your public persona, and it may or may not correspond with your real life persona. I mean, if you are an obnoxious shite then that's probably going to shine through no matter how you try to disguise it. But you are probably a decent enough cove so aim to put your best face forward.

How to get people to follow you
For the first few weeks, you don't need to worry about this. You're not ready for followers yet. Don't worry about the fact that nobody is following you.

So why would anybody follow you?

- **Because they know you.**
  Either they like you or they're being polite. Since Twitter is about connecting with new people, you might find you have less interest in connecting with the people you already know. But at the start, they're the ones who are more likely to follow you so take it where you can get it.

- **Because they find you interesting**
  Maybe they think your tweets are interesting, or they read your blog and are curious about you. Maybe they

work in the same industry.

- **Because they want something from you**

  If you're a journalist specialising in a particular sector, PRs and businesses who want to engage with you will most likely follow you and not expect a follow back. If you say where you live on your profile, businesses in your local area may follow you too.

- **Because they follow everybody back**

  You can tell the people who do this because they generally have equal numbers of followers to people they're following

- **Because you paid them**

  There are services you can use to buy a bunch of followers to instantly bump up your numbers. Bought followers are likely to be false accounts who will not engage with you, won't hire you to write and won't buy your books. Honestly, don't bother.

When to unfollow

Unfollowing people on Twitter is very easy - you can either do it via their profile or by using a cleanup tool like Manageflitter. Go to their profile and hover over where it says Following and click to unfollow. Unless they are using a notification service, they won't know you've gone. Manageflitter lets you unfollow up to 100 people per day so it's a quicker way to do this in bulk.

If you decide to unfollow people who don't follow you back, bear in mind that there are some Twitter feeds you will still want to follow even if they never follow you back. These include industry publications, networking organisations and other relevant sources. Some big brands and organisations have restrictions on who they can follow on Twitter so it's nothing personal.

How to find topics to tweet about
As a writer, this will be easy for you. You can find topics to tweet about from anywhere, either within Twitter or via external research - let's say you read an interesting news article, there'll probably be a button at the bottom to share it on Twitter. Sources for topics to tweet about could come from:

- Publications relevant to your writing niche
- Original material on your website
- General news sites (BBC etc)
- Information about upcoming events

Never tweet or retweet a link without clicking on that link to check where it leads. There are many reasons for this:

- The link might be broken
- It could be an old article (as much as possible avoid tweeting links to anything over a month old)
- It might lead to an article behind a paywall, which your network can't see
- It could be endorsing a client's competitor
- It could simply be far less interesting than the headline promises

Be generous and tweet other writers if you've enjoyed reading something they've written. Think of it as a deposit in the karma bank, or just a nice thing to do.

Respond to anyone who tweets directly @you Not everybody does this, especially if they've got a large following, but it's nice to do as much as you can. Stay connected to people. You'll be glad you did in the long run. If there's an option on your next book, ask your publisher to include your Twitter username so readers can follow you and get in touch.

Hashtags

A hashtag or # sign is a type of label which is used on Twitter to organise content around an event or a topic. It's a sorting system. Don't add any more than three hashtags to any tweet as it will then tend to overwhelm the text. You can use pre-existing hashtags or ones that you make up yourself.

Writers on Twitter can use hashtags in a number of useful ways

- To join in a pre-existing, wider conversation Say everybody's tweeting about X Factor and you want to join in too? Just add #XFactor to the end of your tweet and you're in there.
- To connect with people attending the same event Many conferences and events have an official hashtag and they can be a great way to start your networking before you even leave the house. You could tweet 'Who else is going to #AwesomeConference ? ' And if you're not able to attend an event but you still want to follow the highlights, you can do so by following the hashtag.

- To show that you're a journalist asking a question for an article and not just feeling aimlessly curious, tweet your question or case study request and add the hashtag #journorequest. PRs, on the other hand tend to use #PRrequest. If you then add pls RT (short for Please Retweet) people are more likely to retweet your message in order to help a reporter out.
- To search for information, case studies or experts. Simply put the hashtag into the search box and away you go.

There are no real rules about hashtags and you can always make one up. For example, if I see something that amuses me in my home town of Brighton I may tweet about it using the hashtag #normalforBrighton. When something amazes me, I tend to append #boggles, and if something impresses me a lot then I'll give it #kudos. It's a happy day (for me) when a tweet is worthy of both #boggles and #kudos. I like that stuff the most.

A hashtag is created simply by putting the # symbol in front of a word. Note that there are no spaces in hashtags -if you put in a space then the second word will get disconnected from the #. They usually go at the end of your tweet.

Anyone can make up a hashtag; there isn't an official list. If you are attending an industry event then it's a good idea to ask the organisers if they have assigned a hashtag. You can also search to see who's tweeting about an event and follow them if appropriate.

Relevant hashtags for writers

#amwriting - I must confess that this one gives me THE RAGE. You're not frickin' writing, you're procrastinating on Twitter like the rest of us. There's something a bit smug about it too. Closely related to #amediting which also has the whiff of smug about it too, I reckon. Just get on with the job.

#writingprompts is quite an interesting one to look at if you're feeling a bit of writer's block and are looking for inspiration

#wordcount and #writegoal - used to publicly announce what you plan to get up to and where you're at with your writing. Just remember that nobody probably cares but you, but if it gets the job done then go for it.

#writingtip - worth checking out for your ongoing learning. Whilst many think that writing can't be taught, that's not to say that the professional writer can't always do with learning a few things.

#journorequest - useful when you're looking for case studies or input from brands and PRs

How often to tweet?

This is a question that bothers a lot of novice tweeters, when using Twitter feels like a cumbersome addition to your day. You people need to tweet more often.

Eventually, the flow of Twitter should fit fairly seamlessly into the flow of your day. As I'm writing this at 5pm on a Monday I haven't sent an original tweet to all of my network today. All of my accounts will have tweeted today, as I keep them active via the scheduling tools Hootsuite and Buffer. On my morning tea

break I sent a couple of encouraging @ messages to peo|
saw mentioning that they were scared of driving. I di‹
directly mention my book but they will probably notice it
anyway. And if they don't, that's fine. I'm still glad I
encouraged them. I also spent a little time on Manageflitter and
unfollowed 100 people on one of my accounts that needed a
cleanup, and followed back a few new followers. All of that
took 15 minutes maximum.

Some people find it more useful to have specific times for using
Twitter, especially if they don't have a smartphone to tweet on
the move and are restricted to doing it whenever they crank up
the laptop. I tend to do it when I'm having a cup of tea.
There's a limit to how many cups of tea you can drink in a day,
so it stops it all taking over.

At minimum, tweet a couple of times a day, at least five days a
week. Less people tweet at the weekends, but conversely this
can make it a good time for you to tweet because the
conversation is slower and your tweets are more likely to get
noticed. People are less rushed and have more time to click on
links, so this could be a great time to schedule a link to one of
your books, blog or website.

I honestly couldn't tell you how often I tweet. Some days it's a
little and some days it's a lot. On weekends and holidays it's
hardly at all. Some days like today my conversation is mostly @
other people, so I don't fully broadcast tweets to my whole
network very much.

You do need to allocate time to it, but it doesn't have to take
up your whole day - you can do a lot in 15 minutes a day. But
at the start, getting to grips with Twitter and building your
network will inevitably take more time than that, though still

no more than three to five hours a week.

If it took a lot of time, if it was difficult to do and not fun and useful, people wouldn't do it. It may take a while for you to get through your learning curve and get to a place where you're enjoying Twitter, but stick with it and you'll get there.

Marking favourites

The *Favourites* button is a way of bookmarking tweets you want to refer to later (some tweeters also use it as a way of giving a Thumbs Up to a tweet they enjoyed). When you click on Favourite, Twitter will add that tweet to your list of favourites which should be much shorter than your regular Twitter stream of messages.

Favouriting can be very useful if you're using Twitter to find case studies. Let's say you've sent out a tweet:

Seeking men with 10 cats and a beard for magazine interview #journorequest

The #journorequest hashtag indicates that this is a bona fide journalist's request and not just your personal fetish. You'll undoubtedly get a few hipsters getting in touch, and it's a good idea to file those responses by hitting the Favourite button so they don't get lost in your Twitter stream.

Scheduling tweets

You can either send a tweet straight away, or schedule it to be sent at a later time.

If a major event or tragedy happens which is being widely discussed on Twitter, remember to reschedule your tweets as necessary. You don't want everyone discussing the death of the Queen when up pops your tweet plugging your book about garden sheds which was scheduled for 4pm.

The main scheduling tools most widely in use are Tweetdeck and Hootsuite. Both can be used to manage a number of Twitter accounts at once (though be very careful not to tweet the wrong thing from the wrong account). Both are free and fairly straightforward to use.

Using Twitter remotely via your mobile device
There are a number of different Twitter apps available for smartphones and tablets, but the official Twitter app is a good place to start. It's free, easy to install and can be used to monitor several Twitter feeds at once. It's useful to have remote access as you can then monitor the account and send tweets on the move - perhaps at conferences or networking events.

Don't become one of those bores who's so concerned with tweeting the event they're at that they forget to experience it in real life. Not everything needs to be live-tweeted.

Using Twitter for marketing purposes
Twitter is not a platform designed for direct marketing. People are there for conversation, not to be sold to. You can advertise occasionally, but not too much or it will alienate your network.

If you do decide to advertise or mention services more directly, in general an average of no more than one marketing message per 15 tweets is recommended, and never any more than 20%

of your overall output. So whilst you can directly plug your books, do it sparingly. I do it a little more around Christmas because I figure most people are in a good mood, or drunk.

The best way to use Twitter for marketing purposes is to use it to develop your relationships with people you've already met in real life, or to start relationships with people whom you may later meet. At any business event, if you receive a business card which contains a Twitter handle, connect with that person and say hello to them fairly swiftly. If you are attending an event which has a designated hashtag, use it in advance to connect with others who are also attending.

Hosting a Twitter chat

Or as they're sometimes known, Twitter parties. In these events, which usually take place for an hour, someone hosts and leads with questions or themes, and anyone can join in using a designated hashtag (created and assigned by the host) to show they're taking part. Brands often run these sort of events to support new product launches.

For your Twitter chat to work, it needs to be based around a bigger theme than simply you and your writing. Offer a prize to encourage people to take part - it could be something small like a copy of your book or an Amazon voucher.

Let people know in advance that you'll be doing this - maybe write a short post on your blog or announce it on your Facebook page. It can be a great way to bring your various networks together. Also, this means that anyone who wants to participate but won't be online during the event can pre-schedule some tweets to take part.

Twist a few arms of anyone you know who's very active and has a big following on Twitter to take part. You could ask another author to join you as a co-host. If it sounds complicated, don't be scared because it's not, though neither is it something to do during your first month on Twitter.

And again, if you can run successful Twitter parties for yourself, this is a service you can offer to brands as well. Some tweeters charge big bucks for hosting a Twitter party.

Extra help with Twitter

There are a multitude of apps and programs available to enhance your Twitter experience. Most of them you probably don't need, unless you are running Twitter accounts professionally and need more stats to justify your existence to your client. Whatever you want to do on Twitter - whether it's analyse who your followers are; find out who unfollowed you or which links got the most click throughs, there will be an app to help. A lot of them are free or low cost. The few apps that I do think are useful are listed in the resources section in Chapter 10.

A word of caution though - a lot of the useful free Twitter apps over the last few years have eventually turned into paid for services, or been bought by bigger companies. So don't get too attached to any services you like because it's unlikely to last forever, at least not in a free format. But there's new stuff appearing all the time. Change is good, change is life, change is social media.

Best practice for writers on Twitter

- DON'T BE A DICK
- Start by connecting with the people you know – but don't just make it about chatting with your friends
- Put 'journalist' in your profile (if you are one) and you'll attract more followers
- Don't be boring. Even in 140 characters it's still published writing with your name attached – show yourself as a good writer.
- Look on Twitter as a way to get to know people on a human basis, rather than a pitch for work. People often complain that you need to have contacts to get on in media – well, here is the perfect way to make those contacts.
- Don't pitch via Twitter - it looks amateurish, especially if you get a public knockback. Use it to get to know an editor, then pitch via email and follow up by phone
- Be generous in retweeting other people's links, say thank you if people retweet you
- Be enthusiast about your work and link to anything new you've had published, but don't let it become a bragathon.
- Tweet links to your work and what you're up to e.g. if you're going to an event or conference
- If you're pimping your own published work or blog posts, be sparing and don't do it more than three hours apart

- Use the hashtag #journorequest when you're asking for information, and add please RT
- DON'T BE A DICK. Worth repeating, since really this is all you need to know. Unless you are a dick in real life, in which case there's no hope for you.

Sorry, that was quite a negative note to end on. On a more positive note, follow me on @SocMed4Writers @MediawomenUK and @KidsBlogClub and I will follow you back. On my main account @joannemallon I will follow you back if you tweet to me, so make that your first mission.

3. Facebook

Good for:
- Sharing links, pictures and updates easily
- Connecting in a more meaningful and extended way with people you meet on other social media platforms
- Separating your personal and professional lives
- Online networking

Not so good for:
- Marketing for free - Facebook wants you to pay and will tightly control who sees your updates unless you do.
- Connecting with teens (if they're your audience)
- Terrible time suck.

In this chapter we're looking at:
- Your Facebook ground rules
- How to set up a Facebook page for your writing
- Facebook Edge Rank - what is it and how can you work around it?
- How often to post; how to schedule posts and when to pay for promotion
- How to sell your books on Facebook

Face it, Facebook is huge. Even amongst people who are so over Facebook, it's still widely used and is second only to Google for sheer volume of web traffic. Your readers and editors, publishers, friends and enemies are all on there. So clearly you need to be too.

Facebook has fallen out of favour with some sectors in recent years, specifically the younger generation. Who can blame them really; who wants to be on a network where your mum can comment on your latest hungover ramblings? Or worse, you can comment on your mum's hungover posts. So if your writing is aimed at teenagers then I wouldn't aim too much of your energy at Facebook - the people you want are over on Tumblr and YouTube.

Despite this, it's still mainstream enough not to be ignored. And if you're already on Facebook, and you're unsure about other forms of social media, then expanding it to take in your writing will be easier since you're on a platform that you're already familiar with.

The down side is the huge, huge potential for time suck. You could easily spend hours on Facebook and be no further forward in your writing career. From playing Candy Crush to looking at strangers' wedding photos, you might as well tip your life into a big black hole.

So set some ground rules. These are mine:
- No game playing. I am too old to have time to play Candy Crush. Besides, I already owe at least a month to the Doctor Who version of 2048.
- No clicking on links, especially ones that have very enticing headlines.
- If somebody is boring or annoying me, hide their updates. I'm too chicken to unfriend them, so that'll do for now.

- No need to check all the groups I belong to every time I visit Facebook
- Like Twitter, there's no need to scroll down and try to see every post that appeared since I last logged in.

So take a moment to think about that now - what are your Facebook ground rules? How will you stop yourself from being awarded a gold medal for procrastination?

Why would a writer need a Facebook page?
Facebook now has the option for anyone to run a page or a group, separate from their own personal profile. These used to be called Fan Pages, but then too many of us felt a bit stupid setting up a Fan Page when we were yet to host our own reality TV show, so now they're just called Pages. It means that you can share news of your latest writing with people who are actually interested in it, and not just because they're a blood relation.

What a page like this will do is clearly separate your working, writing life from your personal life. Many of us, if we're self employed find that the personal and the professional tend to blend together quite rapidly. And it used to be that Facebook was only for your real life friends and family – the people you had met face to face and had known for a number of years. But that's not really the case any more, and your Facebook friends are probably a mish mash of family and friends; colleagues and clients; people you know in real life and those you've never met.

You could adjust your privacy settings depending on what you want each person to see of your updates - from fully public to a select group. But that's probably too much of a faff for most people. So if you find that you want to separate out your writing life from your other life on Facebook, creating a page is the way to do it. An individual profile is for you as a person, and a page to represent you as a writer. Most writers whose name goes on their work could benefit from this sort of page. So maybe not commercial copywriters, but definitely journalists and both non-fiction and fiction authors.

You can use your page to showcase your work and build an audience – and as we've noted from the start, this is exactly what editors and publishers are looking for. Facebook is now a major source of traffic for news organisations – The Independent newspaper saw its referrals jump by 680% when it installed a Facebook plugin on its website.

Pages are good for journalists and authors who write features and columns largely based on their own experience, but who still want to keep at least some of their private life private. You may also have sources that you want to keep in contact with, but not necessarily be close friends with. A page lets you have that connection without giving too much access to your personal details.

And you can spread your network as far as you like - a page allows you to have unlimited connections by allowing any number of 'likes', whereas personal profiles have a limit of 5000 friends.

Other benefits to having a Facebook page for your writing
- Use it to source information and interviewees, particularly case studies
- You can post extra photos if you're travelling on a story. Maybe only one or two photos will make it into

the final feature, and the rest could become an album on Facebook as extra value for your readers.

- Use it as a two way conversation – ask questions, encourage debate. If you've got an idea for a pitch or book proposal, you can use Twitter and Facebook as a testing ground to see if your idea strikes a chord

If you want to tag another person or page in your update, use the @ symbol before their name. That way they will get a notification that they've been tagged, and may even share your update to their network. So say you've written a feature that quotes some other people or references a particular business - tag them when you share. If they share to their page fans, it could mean more traffic for your article, which will make you more popular with your editor. You can only tag someone if you are friends with them, but you can tag any public page.

Social media as writers use it:

Alexandra Robbins @AlexndraRobbins
Alexandra Robbins is the New York Times bestselling author of the upcoming book: "THE NURSES: A Year with the Heroes Behind the Hospital Curtain". She runs a really terrific Facebook page https://www.facebook.com/AuthorAlexandraRobbins which shows how to connect meaningfully with your readers.

Alexandra says "I love interacting with my readers. Book writing can be a solitary life, and my Facebook page is an excellent antidote to that professional loneliness. On that page, as well as my public

Facebook friend page, I simply aim to interact with people. The pages aren't really about promoting my books; they are about connecting with, sharing with, and learning from friends and strangers. Via social media, I have "met" some great people, found fascinating sources, and rallied people to come to another individual's aid.

"Last week I posted a (non-identifying) email from a high school student who was distraught because she was the new girl at school and her classmates were mistreating her. I asked for advice I could give her in addition to my own. Within minutes, several people responded with wonderful insights, which I forwarded back to the girl. The next day, the girl wrote me to say that the advice worked and that thanks to my Facebook readers, she had experienced a 180-degree turnaround at school; she had even used someone's specific tip to make a new friend. Can't beat that!"

How to set up a Facebook Page for your writing

This is incredibly easy. Simply look at the left hand column when you're logging in to Facebook and you'll see a button called Create a Page. Click that and you're away. From there, you've got a number of options and extras you can add in, and you can make it as simple or complex as you like.

Facebook offers a number of categories, and most of the time you want the one called Artist, Band or Public Figure. Yes I know it's a little odd to think of yourself as a public figure, but go with it. This is the you that your readers will see. Possibly with a better haircut and shinier shoes, but it's still you.

The other option that might be relevant to some writers is to create a Facebook community, if you envisage your page being a place that people come to chat. This would take a lot more admin time from you, but it could work very well for some sorts of books and groups, so think about whether that might work for you. For example, the beauty writer Sali Hughes had a very successful discussion group on her Facebook page, who then came with her when she launched her website and who are probably buying her book right now.

So you could have a community, but a page is more likely to work better for most authors. You can launch as many pages for free as you want to, so it's entirely possible to have a separate page or community for each book you publish. However, if your books are in a similar genre or are part of a series then it will simplify things considerably if you just keep them together on one page. It may seem like an enormous achievement to have written a book, as indeed it is, but hopefully you won't just ever write one book. If you think or hope that the same sorts of people will read them all, best keep it all together. For me, I've got one book about parenting and another one about fear of driving so although they're both self help, there's not a lot of crossover for readers there. Possibly they needed a page each, although what actually happened was that I chickened out, didn't do one for either and opted to focus on Twitter instead.

Other Facebook options if you don't want a page
Another option on Facebook, if you don't fancy running a page and write under a different name, is to have a separate profile under your writing name, or a version of it, and only connect with people in a professional capacity on that account.

I must admit I was quite miffed once when I realised that a writer I had thought I was friendly with turned out to have two Facebook profiles under her maiden and married names. The maiden name was also her byline name, so this profile was very work focused, and was kept for case study shout outs and showing off her latest published features. The married name profile, I guess, was for her real friends and contained more personal stuff. Yes I am being a big baby at being miffed at not being as close to the inner circle than I thought I was, but at least when there's a page for your writing versus a profile, everybody knows what's what.

I suspect it's easier to manage as well. You can't be logged in to two profiles at the same time from the same computer, whereas you can manage a page when you're logged in under your usual profile. This ease of use is another reason I'd recommend profile plus page. That and you lessen the risk of upsetting big babies like me.

Or you can stick with your regular personal profile, but tinker with the privacy settings to segregate your Facebook friends into lists of different interests - say one for close friends, another for family, another for writing buddies etc. Then when you post an update, you can choose which list sees it. It's very similar to the different circles option we will see on Google Plus.

However, nothing is ever truly private on the internet, and especially not on Facebook, so the golden rule remains that if you don't want people to see it, don't post it. Let's say you write about adult themes, but you have some really uptight relatives you don't want to know about it - yes you could attempt to restrict what they know by not connecting with them on Facebook, or restricting what they see, but these things don't tend to end well. Publishing what you write, under your name, means taking what you create out into the public space, and at that point you lose control over who reads it and knows about it. Which is fine really - we all need our audiences to spread beyond the people we personally know, unless you want to have really really tiny book sales. So don't be afraid. The people who love you will still love you after they've read what you've written. In most cases, anyway.

Putting your page together
First of all, look at some of the Facebook pages maintained by other writers you like. How do they run them? What do you like and what do you not like?

To launch your Facebook page you'll need to fill in all the various sections with a bit of blurb about who you are. You'll also need a header image - the landscape picture that goes across the top of the page. Spend time creating this image - it needs to be 851 pixels wide by 315 pixels deep. Smaller than this and the image may not upload, or it may become stretched across the page and look very odd. For your header image, a spread of your books or cuttings, or a collage of you in action can work well. At minimum, select something that chimes in with the rest of what you do, perhaps a reference to your most recently published work, or the last event you appeared at. You can change this banner more frequently than you might do your individual profile page, so have it represent whatever you're currently plugging. You'll find some resources in the back of the book for easy ways to create banner images using online tools such as Picmonkey.

You'll need a small profile pic as well - probably your headshot, and almost certainly the same photo you use across the rest of social media.

No one will see your page unless they click the Like button to see its updates, so make the most of this time when no one's watching. Fill up a few photo albums - anything goes as long as it's relevant to your writing.

Although the purpose of your page is to promote you as a writer, that doesn't mean that it has to be all about you. Link to news stories that interest you or charities and events you support. Promote other people as much as you promote yourself. Like all of life, it's about give and take and you will have to start giving before you can take. Think about what else your page fans might be interested in. This is where you can save yourself some time by reusing material you've curated. So say you read a great article online that you think people who like your work would be interested in - that can be shared on your Twitter, Facebook page, G+ and LinkedIn. Just not all at once, and not using the same language to introduce it. Each platform has a distinct tone of voice, so whilst you might be more serious on LinkedIn, you can play fast and loose with the cat jokes on Facebook.

You don't have to post to your page every day, though if you want to you could start with daily then pull back to three-ish times a week. Enough for people to remember you, but not so much that they get sick of you. As you add updates, experiment with picture only, links, text plus links and text only. Shorter updates/posts usually perform better. Include a call to action as often as you can. No need to post an extract from your novel.

Once you've got a few likes, you can also reach out and use your page to like other pages of anyone connected to your writing, and leave comments on their updates. To toggle between using Facebook as you, and using it as your page, look along the top of the page when you're logged in. On the far right of the dark blue section you'll see a small triangle that looks like an arrow pointing down. Click on this and it will give you the option to use Facebook as you, or as your page, or any other page you're registered as an Admin for. This is particularly useful if you're running a number of Facebook pages, which you might end up doing if you get into social media management work. Don't forget to toggle back again when you want to revert to your regular identity. It's easier than Superman reverting to Clark Kent status, though less fun.

When you're ready to unleash your page to the public, let people know through your other social media channels that you've set up a page. Don't be offended if people you thought were your friends don't 'like' your Facebook page. Most of us get multiple requests to do this and it's easy to miss.

You could even host an online release party when your book is released. And if you're having a real life release party for your book, Facebook can be a great way to manage the event and invite people, plus add in an album full of photos of the event afterwards. Extending your real life activities into your social media network like this can be a great way to help fans of your writing feel part of your world and community.

Making your page look lived in

Facebook pages now have a timeline feature, so you can go back in time and post about significant milestones. The advantage of this is that it makes it look like your page has a bit of longevity to it, rather than being something you just threw together last Thursday. So think about what sort of events might be suitable to put into your timeline. Books being

published is an obvious one, but you could also inclu(
awards you've been nominated for, or events you spoke
simply something cool that happened a few years ago. It all
make you look like a writer of substance, who's lived a life and
is worth paying attention to. That's the idea, anyway.

To set a Milestone, go to the status update box where you
would normally write a post. Click on *Offer,Event+* and when
that pops up, you'll see the option to set a Milestone too, at
whatever date you like.

Pinning Posts
You can also pin a published update to the top of your page
(Twitter also has this function, where you can pin a tweet to
the top of your profile). To pin an update, hover over the top
of the right hand corner of the box where you've written your
post. A small downward arrow will appear, with a number of
options under it including Pin To Top. You might want to do
this if there's something you particularly want page fans to see,
like news of a new event or publication. To unpin a post, hover
over the same place and you'll see the Unpin option appear.

Highlighting posts
This is another little visual tool to help ensure that more people
see your updates. All it does is make your update bigger than
the other updates on the page, so use it sparingly for maximum
impact. If an update is getting a lot of interaction and
comments then it can be worth doing this to ensure it gets even
more. Or if your update includes a particularly striking image
that will look good nice and big on the page, go for it.

The highlight option is another one that appears when you hover over the top right hand corner of your posts. While we're here, this is the same button you want if you are creating a time-limited special offer or an event you want to invite people too.

By the way, don't expect a Facebook event invitation to be enough for your book launch if you really want people to be there. Many people simply don't see the private messages and event invitations they receive on Facebook. So if there are people you really want to be there, be aware that you'll have to contact them another way too - the more old school they are, the more old school you'll have to be when you contact them.

Social media as writers use it:

John Higgs @johnhiggs
John Higgs is author of *The KLF: Chaos, Magic and the Band who Burned a Million Pounds* and *Stranger Than We Can Imagine: Making Sense of the Twentieth Century*. Whilst he doesn't want to have a Facebook page for his writing, he reluctantly maintains one, though his heart remains with Twitter: "I'm not a fan of Facebook and use it begrudgingly. I set up an 'author' page, thinking that I could keep my 'personal' page for family and old friends, but I find I get as many friend requests from readers to my personal page as I do likes on my author page. I think that's in part because Facebook only shows your page updates to a fraction of your likers – your official page doesn't travel over the network in the same way your personal page does. As a result I have to put important announcements on both pages, which seems a little

spammy. I'm not comfortable with this as I'm the first to click 'hide' on Facebook friends who over-post.

"What I don't like about Facebook is the way it selects what is visible in your news feed. It seems overly keen on news stories that you saw on Twitter a few days ago. When you do spot something interesting, you can't think, 'oh I'll look at that later' because it could be removed from your feed and you'll never find it again. I also removed the Facebook app from my phone after an update requested permission to read all my text messages. I don't trust the company, basically. But I continue to use Facebook because that is where everybody is. At the moment, anyway."

Settings on your Facebook page

Facebooks offers plenty of options for what you can do and what other people can do on your page. You'll find them under the Settings tab at the top of the page (only you and anybody else you appoint as Page Admin will be able to see these administrative tabs. Everybody else just sees the page). Keep these settings fairly open, unless you are in hiding from someone or have plans to run a dictatorship. If this is the case then Facebook is most likely not the best place for you anyway.

So it's yes to letting other people post on your page, or tag you in posts, or send you private messages. There's a profanity filter, and you have the option to ban certain words, but if your readers are adults (and if they're on Facebook then in theory they should be at least 13) then hopefully you won't need this.

Obviously if you did start to get hit by spammers or trolls/online bullies then you might want to lock some of that stuff down but that's highly unlikely to happen, and in the worst case scenario, if it did, it's easy to change. You can also block individuals by name from seeing your page, though if they are really determined there's nothing to stop them opening up another Facebook account and liking your page under that.

Have a play about with these settings before you show your page to the world. Check that you are happy with the default settings as they stand, and that you know what you are and are not able to do.

You can appoint anyone else as administrator to your page, and this can be useful if you think it needs keeping an eye on and you're not going to be able to do it. But be aware that this is a big ask and it's something that people usually do as a job. Whining that you're not technically minded enough to do it is not an excuse, because this is not a technically challenging job.

If anything, with a Facebook page, the challenge is a combination of psychology and writing skills - noticing what sort of updates your audience responds to and thinking about how you can build on that.

If you've got a smartphone or tablet/iPad, then the Facebook Pages Manager app is well worth downloading because this can be used to update your page on the go, and will also notify you if someone leaves a comment on your page. You can also choose to be notified via email if you prefer.

Tabs on your page
You can create up to 12 custom tabs on your page, but only four will be visible at any one time, and these can be seen under your banner image. You can then change them around and

decide in what order they appear. These tabs link to pages which each have their own URL, so you could use each of them to promote individual books or events.

Getting people to like your page

This is the fun part, and where all your social media platforms start to coalesce. So if you use Twitter, tweet about it. If you're a blogger, blog about it. It can be a struggle at first to attract likes because the world and her wife seems to have a Facebook page already. So you might have to tell people more than once, to get through the noise. I am more than happy to like my friends' pages, but I need to know about them and I don't always see the notifications because so many get sent every day.

As soon as you've created your page, Facebook will prompt you to ask everyone you're already connected with to like it. Resist the temptation to do this straight away. One way to start could be to tell people via a status update on your usual profile that you've started a page dedicated to your writing, and ask anyone who's interested to like it. That way you're asking people to raise their hands in a softer way than with individual invitations.

Facebook moves so fast that many people who might be interested in your page might not see your initial update, so maybe send out a few invitations a week or two later. But don't send them to everyone indiscriminately. Go through your list and only invite those you think might have a legitimate reason for being interested in your writing. People who have their own pages are usually a good bet, because they'll know that it can be a challenge to attract likes. Make sure you return the favour and like their page too. Be as generous in liking other people's pages as you hope they will be to yours.

Other things you could do to promote your Facebook page include:

- Adding it to your automatic signature so people you email will see it
- Adding it to your business cards. Give people a choice as to how they want to keep in touch with you.
- Add a Facebook plug in to your website

Scheduling posts

The scheduling button on Facebook is worth seeking out because it's one of the most useful features. It helps you make great use of your time because you can schedule multiple updates at once.

On your page, click on the status box (the bit that says 'What have you been up to?'). Write your status as normal, adding in any links or pictures as you normally would. Then click on the downward arrow next to Post and the scheduling option will pop up (along with Backdate and Save as Draft). Add in the time and date you want your status to publish, click Schedule and you're all done.

You can schedule posts up to six months in advance, though I can't think why you'd want to. It's more useful if you're going to be away for a few weeks and want to keep the page current, or if you are organising your Facebook admin time into one block.

As with scheduled Twitter posts, it's very important to remember what you've scheduled and go back fairly soon so you can deal with any engagement. If a fan leaves a comment you don't want to leave them hanging for a week for an answer - this is where the Pages Manager app is very handy because it tells you straight away when someone comments. Also, watch out for big news events that might render your scheduled posts obsolete. You don't want to be the dork that pops up in everybody's timeline babbling about your latest release if everybody else is focusing on the latest world tragedy.

Beware of Edge Rank

One important point that you need to be aware of is that Facebook purposely limits who sees the posts on your page, using an algorithm called Edge Rank.

Say you have a Facebook page for your writing, and 100 people have clicked the Like button. It would be reasonable to expect that if you put an update on your page, then those 100 people would see it. Not so. Facebook restricts the number of 'likers' who will see your post to around 10% of the total. So maybe 10-13 of your likers will have your post show up in their news feed, and if they don't happen to be online then they might not see it at all.

Essentially, what Facebook wants is for you to pay for the rest of your network to see your update. This is why you'll see prompts popping up on your account urging you to promote your post so that more people see it.

Facebook has come under criticism in recent years for this squeezing out of who gets to see a page's posts, but the bottom line is that it is a money making organisation, not a free marketing platform.

There are all sorts of theories about how you can outsmart Edge Rank, but the truth is that nobody really knows. Facebook certainly isn't telling, because then there would be no reason for us to pay. I think it is worth paying to promote your posts when you are first getting into launching your page, say to get you past the first 100 'likers' so your page doesn't look too lonely, or if you have something special to promote like a new book launch.

One of the theories behind Edge Rank goes that if a post on your page was popular (popularity being measured by interaction, ie how many people 'liked' it or left a comment), then Edge Rank will allow more people to see your next post or update.

This is why you see posts on Facebook from brands along the lines of 'Click Like if you love kittens' - they're looking for lots of people to like the post, so that when the brand sends out their next marketing post, more people will get to see it without the brand having to pay Facebook to promote their posts.

Unless you are managing a Facebook page for a company you don't have to worry too much about Edge Rank, as attempting to outsmart it will tend to fry the brain. But do be aware that only a small amount of the people who like your page will ever get to see the posts you put on it. So experiment with ways to reach those people, and particularly pay attention to the times of day you post and what gets the best interaction. I often think that outside office hours can be a good time, because this is not when brands tend to post, so there'll be less noise to get in the way.

Paying to promote your posts on Facebook

Ultimately, this is what Facebook would really, really like you to do. This is why they have Edge Rank to restrict the number of people who will see your page for free.

If you do decide to put some budget into promoting your posts, it doesn't have to be a lot. It could be as little as $5. You can also specify who you want to promote by language, age and location. So say you have a romance novel being published in France - you can reach out directly to people who might be interested.

If it's something big that doesn't come around often, then putting a bit of budget into promoting it is worth considering. The down side is that at least some of the people who see your sponsored post might not like it. Obviously it would be great if we got all the interaction we needed for free on Facebook, but the company deliberately ensures that this doesn't happen.

Analysing your Facebook statistics

If you're finding the simple business of running your Facebook page cumbersome, you may not want to go much further in terms of analysing what's happening on your page, but if you do it will help you to use your page more effectively.

You can't do this sort of analysis with a personal profile - another reason why pages are more useful for people with something to promote. When you click on your Facebook page, look for a tab at the top of the page called Insights. Click on this and you'll see lots of stats about your page - how many new likes, how many people saw your posts and engaged with them (by sharing, liking or leaving a comment) etc. There's also the option to 'watch' similar pages to your own to compare

...ance with yours, though frankly this seems a bit ...que and not really necessary for most of us.

...f you are running your own page then the Insights section is useful for a broad overview of how well (or not) your posts are going down - look at which posts get seen by the most people and which ones lead to the most engagement, then think about how you can do more of the same.

If you are running a page for someone else then you will have to learn how to use the information here in more detail, probably to create reports for your clients. This is where you justify your job and get better at it by analysing how well your posts are doing.

Insights will also provide a breakdown of your page demographics - how many of your fans are male or female; where they live; what's their main language. So for example if you're in the UK but a high proportion of your page fans are in the USA then you might want to schedule your updates to fit in with US timezones. Post when more people are awake and you stand more chance of them seeing your posts.

Only you and anyone you appoint as admin can see the Insights page, so take some time to click on the various tabs and consider the information available. Most of it you won't need, so don't let yourself get overwhelmed by it. The time it really comes in handy is if you ever pay to promote something on Facebook and you want to check the results to see if you got what you were after. And if you're a freelancer and think you might want to add running Facebook pages to the services you offer, all knowledge is good.

How often and when to post on your Facebook page?

How often depends on how often you have something new to say - you might be running a giveaway on your blog, or have a newly published article to tell people about, or be canvassing opinions for something you're writing.

For most pages, updating once a day is plenty - aim for two to five times a week. The types of content which generally get the most interactions are pictures, videos and questions. So a picture of a cat with a funny face asking what's for dinner is always going to do well.

If you upload a picture or a video then Facebook will show it to more people than it would if you simply posted the link via an outside website - it's an Edge Rank thing. Because Facebook doesn't want people going to outside websites, it wants people on its own sites, looking at its content and hopefully clicking on its ads. It didn't get to be such a horrendous time suck by accident.

Put simply - if you go to Facebook.com and log into your account to share an update, Facebook will put that update in front of more eyeballs than it would if you were to share it from another site. So always update from within Facebook itself, rather than clicking on 'Share to Facebook' buttons or using an automatic system such as Buffer or ITTT (more on these systems in the last chapter).

One way you can make your posts stand out more is to upload an image plus the website address you want people to click on, rather than simply pasting in the URL and letting Facebook automatically pick up a thumbnail image. It's a bit more fiddly, but if you upload the picture separately then it appears slightly bigger and stands out a bit more in readers' newsfeeds. This means that readers are more likely to see it and then hopefully interact with it by clicking, commenting, reading etc.

How to sell your books on Facebook
You can't do this if you only have a personal profile, but if you have a fan page then various apps exist to help you set up a virtual 'storefront' on your page.

The down side to this is that it will inevitably make your page immediately seem more commercial, and people may be put off liking your page if they think there's going to be too much hard sell. Although the page is a marketing tool in itself, there's a big difference between occasional book mentions and Amazon links, and a permanent ad. People don't really tend to use Facebook to make purchases directly yet. But if it interests you, and you think it could work for your audience, play around with it - maybe experiment with one of these services for a month or so and see how it goes. Tell your page fans that this is what you're doing - could make for an interesting dialogue!

Facebook shop apps vary a lot - most have an entry level free version. Do your research to see which is the best regarded if you're going to try one out. At the moment this feels to me like an area that might develop in the future, so it's worth keeping an eye on, but it's a long way from mainstream take up.

Final thoughts on Facebook
Facebook changes its settings and terms constantly, and it doesn't usually advertise these changes. You, the user, need to keep on top of that stuff. Find out where the Privacy settings are and get to know how to use them.

The main thing to remember with Facebook is that it's not a free platform set up so you can chat to your friends and market your writing or any other services. There is a cost to using it - everything you click on is monitored and will affect your future experience. Just as you may monitor how people engage with your fan page, so somebody somewhere is monitoring how you engage with the service as a whole, and money is being made off the back of that.

But it can still be an enjoyable and useful experience, and as a writer I know that Facebook has served me well. I've used it to get to know people who ended up hiring me. I've had work running Facebook pages for clients. I've had lots of media interviews to promote my books via belonging to writers' groups on Facebook. I've been able to network with lots of great writers and find out what they wanted from a book like this. But as with all social media I am cautious with what I give away - minimal photos and not that many public updates. I participate in a lot of Facebook blogging groups. This puts me in touch with a variety of people and means I'm well placed to source case studies.

I don't do many public status updates, maybe once a week if even that. If I've had something published I might link to that. What I do much more of is interact with other people - leaving comments and having conversations. The reason for this is partly one of time - I prefer to use my time on Twitter and blogging. But also there's a certain shyness coming in to play - everyone from my kids to my elderly relatives are now on Facebook and I don't necessarily want them to see what I'm up to all the time. I don't want them to feel like an audience I'm marketing to.

I think this is why I'm getting into Google Plus a lot more these days. It feels fresher, plus I can avoid all the people I'm trying to avoid on social media. Right now, hardly anyone I know actively uses Google Plus. Let's go break new ground.

4. Google Plus

Good for:
- Getting your links and site ranked higher on the Google search engine
- Creating video content via Hangouts
- Avoiding all the people who bore you on Facebook
- Anyone who likes a slower moving pace of social media

Not so good for:
- Large scale web traffic (depending on topic)
- Connecting with the mainstream
- Ease of use - other platforms are much easier to understand quickly

In this chapter we're looking at:
- What is Google Plus and why do I need to be there?
- How to complete your Google Plus profile
- What to post to Google Plus
- How and why to create Google Hangouts

What is Google Plus and why should I care?
Now, Google Plus is a funny old beast. For every person who thinks it's the future of social media, there are many more who've either never heard of it, or have heard of it and think it's a graveyard.

But there's one reason you need to take at least a sideways glance at Google Plus - as the name suggests, it's a Google product. Essentially it's Google's answer to Facebook, and as more people have turned off Facebook in recent years, G+ has made gains in certain sectors. Also, if you want to be found via the Google search engine then actively using G+ will help this to happen. Any link which you share on G+ will do better on Google searches than if you didn't, even if you have very few G+ connections and nobody really sees it or leaves a comment. This is the single benefit of G+ which makes it worth paying attention to.

You know when you see the options for social media shares on an online article? Articles that are shared more often via G+ will then turn up higher in Google searches. And the higher you can do that the better, since most people don't tend to look beyond the first page or two of Google when searching. This is why some editors (especially for websites and online editions of print publications) love it, and will welcome a writer who's active on G+. The assumption is that what you write will get shared more on G+ and therefore their whole site will do better in search engine rankings. So yes, in certain situations it can definitely pay to be popular on G+. Though there are still plenty of editors who will back away from it in horror. It's not a universally popular asset.

Since Google products are now linked up together, and Google also owns YouTube, if you leave a comment on YouTube it will also show up in your G+ feed. If you have a Gmail account then you will automatically have a G+ profile, even if you don't want it and never use it. This feature has recently been made optional for new Gmail accounts, but for those of us who already have Gmail it applies.

Some Blogger blogs also now have G+ commenting systems (the blog platform Blogger is also a Google product), meaning that conversations can expand from a blog into G+ quite easily. Basically, Google really really wants us all to be using G+ and is using every asset at its disposal to get us there.

But still, some people think that G+ is an endangered beast because despite all of this promotion it has failed to reach the mass market in the way Twitter and Facebook have. Do you know anyone that actively uses it?

Google has invested millions of dollars and working hours into G+ so I don't think they're about to dump it in a hurry. Personally, I think that they will jump either way within the next six months - either they'll keep tinkering (which will most likely mean simplifying and making it look pretty) until it reaches mass take up; or they'll pull down the shutters and walk away.

So whilst I don't think G+ is yet at the point where it's worth investing a huge amount of your time, it's still worth keeping an eye on. How close that eye is depends on your writing niche. As a minimum, fill out your profile completely. The G+ profile page includes a section to add in anywhere you write for regularly, and you can also add in an Amazon link to any published works.

Social media as writers use it:

Emma Cossey @emma_cossey
Emma Cossey is a freelance writer and freelance lifestyle coach. She's also a real pioneer when it comes to all things social media, and as such she's found

herself turning to G+ instead of Twitter: "Google+ is excellent for crowdsourcing, and I've had some really intelligent, well thought out responses on there. I also find it crucial for holding and saving interviews, using the Google+ Hangout Live function (saving to YouTube), and for virtual meetings. It's a whole new community, sitting somewhere between Facebook and LinkedIn in that it's professional but you have a bit more creative freedom on there.

"You can share work projects, events you've been to or personal blog posts, but you avoid the really personal, passive aggressive tone that Facebook can have. For writers, it's really useful for crowdsourcing, and I've used it on several occasions to have Hangouts Live with other writers and freelancers to discuss projects or topics. I actually think its lack of mainstream appeal is a benefit - those that use it tend to be more focused and clear about what they're posting, and happier to get involved with intelligent debate. Twitter has a tendency to just be a stream of self-promotion at the moment, and Google+ is a breath of fresh air in comparison."

However, this doesn't mean that Emma has abandoned other forms of social media, especially when it comes to promotion: "I usually go for my Facebook page first, followed by Pinterest, Twitter and Instagram. I'm still hoping that Instagram will introduce clickable links! For all social media, my advice to newbies is to read as much as you can elsewhere, and get involved with others. Twitter is a great place to start, as it's full of writers, journalists, bloggers and editors. Follow people you like the look of, check out the suggested people section, tweet others and retweet. Essentially, put in what you want to get out of it".

Who uses Google Plus?

In October 2013, Google claimed that there were 540 million active users who used at least one Google+ service, of which 300 million users are active G+ users. On paper at least, it's the second largest social networking site next to Facebook. Another reason not to ignore it, even if all those people are keeping remarkably quiet and certainly not showing up on my feed.

Statistically, those users are mainly men, who outnumber women two to one, with the dominant age bracket between 25-34. So if youngish techy guys are who you're aiming to connect with (for whatever reason) this is where they are.

Your G+ profile

Whilst this is the section to take most care over, it shouldn't take too long to fill out the profile section and you can probably reuse some of the stuff you wrote for other networks. It doesn't have to be as serious as LinkedIn, although the profile does follow a similar format of listing your achievements. As such it will need to be updated every once in a while, as you achieve more cool stuff.

A profile or a page?

In G+ terms, you have a choice between having a profile or a page. Profiles are for people and pages are for businesses and brands. You as an individual can have one profile, but you can manage more than one page from there. You could have a page your blog, but you're probably fine to stick with one personal profile for you and your blog and other published writing. Whilst on Facebook it makes sense to have a separate page for your writing, I don't think G+ is well-used enough as a network to make this necessary for individual writers. You could create a page for a new book or project, but this is another thing for you to manage - do you really have time to do that?

Be aware of pages and the fact that you might want one some day. Nobody had separate fan pages on Facebook until a few years ago, and Google Plus is at that stage now. So I don't think most of us need pages right now, unless we're running one for a client. The exception to this would be if you are writing something aimed at very tech savvy American men. Those guys you will find on G+, so throw something their way.

Additionally, if you are offering Social Media Management professionally then it makes sense to know about pages and how to run them. In fact, if you do work like this then the more you know about G+ the better as it's not widely understood yet, so this will help you stand out professionally from the crowd.

In theory you can do quite a lot with pages, and there's some stuff you can do with profiles that you can't do with pages. But this is where Google Plus starts to trip itself up and become over-complicated. And it's the over-complicated nature of G+ that has stopped mass take-up, so I think those things will be the first to go.

Google Hangouts

Google Hangouts are one of the best features of G+, and the one that's most likely to be of use to you. Essentially they are like a group Skype video call that you can record and share instantly on YouTube. This creates a video that you can then share on your blog, Facebook page or wherever you like.

The first time I did a Google Hangout, my children, who are usually extremely uninterested in how I spend my days, did actually show a small amount of interest, saying *Google Hangouts are cool. Barack Obama's done a Google Hangout.* Well OK then, it's clearly worth spending time on.

Google Hangouts can include a maximum of 10 people, so that's you and nine others. The person who's speaking is shown in the main, larger picture, with everyone else as small thumbnails along the bottom of the screen. When a person speaks, their image zips up to the top so they're the main picture. As such it gets a bit confused if anybody taking part has a persistent cough. You need to be quiet if you're not speaking. It's not a free for all, and it helps if somebody acts as chairperson. I found a hangout particularly useful when I was speaking on a panel at a conference, and we had a pre-conference meeting to discuss what we'd like to talk about. It's a great way to host a face to face meeting with people who are geographically spread.

You could use this tool for all sorts of things - host a virtual book group with your readers, or an online networking discussion. Use it for video conference calls if you're working remotely with a client, to interview a source or create content for your website.

Hangouts can be totally private, so only the people taking part will see them, and they don't all have to end up on YouTube. Or you can open them up and live stream them on G+ or on your website. They're very easy to set up and get going - if you're unsure, practise doing one by yourself before launching into a hangout with a client.

G+ Communities
Communities on G+ vary a lot and are often much less active than comparable Facebook groups. When you join a community, make sure you turn off the little bell on the community page, otherwise you will be getting an email every time somebody posts to the group. Check out how active a group is before you join. You won't get much action in a graveyard.

G+ fans claim that whilst the quantity may be less, the quality of conversation is higher. I do think that G+ communities could be an untapped source of riches as far as sourcing interviewees and case studies is concerned. Get in there before all the other journalists do.

The +1 button
You've probably seen the +1 button as a social sharing option on articles on the internet. It's the equivalent to liking something on Facebook or sharing it on Twitter, except less people will see it. It's an easy way to endorse something you've read and share it with your G+ network. And each time you do this, whatever you recommended gets a little higher bump in Google's search engine. So use this button generously and don't forget to +1 your own stuff too.

Google+ Ripples

This feature shows an interactive graph of anything you posted and how it 'rippled' throughout your social media network. It's useful for tracking how far a message went and which messages resonate most with your audience. Whether or not you want to do this depends how much time you find you're spending on G+. Just because you can track something doesn't mean you always need to, and sometimes stuff like this is just an extra thing to take up space in your head when you could be writing.

Circles on G+

The big advantage of G+ over Facebook is that you can segment your network via circles much more easily, and choose who you want to see your updates. And if you post an update or link, the people you want to see it stand a higher chance of actually doing so, with no pesky algorithm restricting who sees what and asking you to pay so more people can see it.

You may choose to segment your connections depending on what you're there for and who you want to reach. Choose your circles when you start, before you have too many connections, as it's a lot easier than trying to segment people later on.

My biggest circle on G+ is called Blogging Friends, and this includes the many people I know in the blogging world. I also have a circle for Acquaintances, which includes people I know online and have also met in real life. If I know them any better than that then I figure we're already connected on Facebook. I also have a circle for Family & Friends, but that only includes my partner and children - essentially the people who live in my house, apart from the cat. And finally there's a circle called Media which includes editors, publications etc.

When you name a circle, only you know what that circle's called. People will get a notification if you've added them to a circle, but they won't know that that circle is called Whiny People Who Suck.

If someone circles you on G+, you don't have to circle them back, though if you know them then it would be nice to do so. The etiquette is much more akin to Twitter than Facebook, in that a lot of the time it's strangers connecting with strangers and then becoming friends (or not, if it turns out they've nothing in common). Since the connections are looser, they're more easily undone, but it's no big deal if somebody uncircles you, or if you uncircle them.

G+ users can also share circles with each other, so you can find more people to connect with quickly. You can create multiple circles, move contacts amongst them and share them with your contacts.

What sort of stuff to update?
Posting an update to G+ is much the same as posting to any network, though that doesn't mean you should post exactly the same sort of stuff. G+ is very visual, in that the pictures show up much bigger than they do on Facebook and Twitter, so prioritise sharing anything with striking visuals.

For most people, their G+ stream (the equivalent of your news feed on Facebook) moves much slower than that of other networks, which may suit you just fine since it's easier to keep up. This also makes it easier to build relationships, since there's less constant chatter. And you don't have to post too often to have an active page.

When you post an update to G+, you might notice a tick box that gives you the option to email all your circles and let them know you've updated.

NEVER TICK THE BOX

Seriously, never ever do this. It pisses people off immensely. Imagine if you got an email each time someone you know updated Facebook? How annoying would that be? Well, that's what this feature offers. Hopefully it will be gone soon.

I've heard people justify using this function by saying that their update was, like, really, really important. But what is important to you is not the same definition as what is important to me, and it's quite arrogant to assume otherwise. Only tick the box if it's a life or death situation, and even then not always.

Google Authorship

Just to show you the speed at which these things change, when I started writing this chapter Google Authorship was vitally important for writers, as it was increasingly being used by mainstream publishers. By the time I had finished, Google Authorship had been dumped.

What was it? It's got nothing to do with being an author. This tool was about connecting all the bits and pieces you write on the web, including your blog, and crediting them as being written by you, with a little photo byline at the side.

So with authorship set up, if someone then Googled your name, they'd see a small headshot and a list of your links. In fact, any of your links would appear in search engine results with the little headshot, and this made them stand out more and therefore be more likely to be clicked on. You can see why it was popular with many websites.

But for reasons best known to itself, Google dumped this feature in August 2014 - something to do with streamlining the user experience. That, and the fact that when people are searching on tiny phone screens, your lovely headshot was taking up too much space. So, goodbye one of the features of G+ that was useful for writers.

It's moves like this that make many commentators speculate that Google is becoming less committed to G+, and is slowly but surely backing away from it. I think we'll know for sure within the next year. So for now, keep an eye on proceedings but don't feel you have to fully commit to the team.

At the time of writing...
The jury is still out on how popular Google Plus will prove to be in the long run, but Google as a company isn't going anywhere, so my bet is that whilst it might change a lot (and it needs to, to get people to use it), it's not going to disappear.

The good part about it right now is that since it's an emptier room, you can make a bigger noise. You can be the one to start up and lead communities, and inevitably raise your profile.

The main problem with G+ as far as I can see is that it isn't particularly user friendly, and it has too many features. It feels like a bit of a mess. No wonder people are put off, especially given that we live in an age where nobody reads instruction manuals and technology is generally pretty easy to pick up intuitively. Twitter has succeeded through being super simple. Google Plus is a lot more complicated than that, although possibly they're appealing to people who want that.

In a way, the fact that it's still on the fringes can be a plus point. Use it for research and you'll almost certainly find different material than you would elsewhere. Even though it's not mainstream, it's still big. So if you find the likes of Twitter and Facebook far too fast paced, maybe you could be one of the pioneers of Google Plus instead.

But if you prefer a more traditional approach, with less gratuitous pictures of cats, come with me now on a journey through time and space and LinkedIn.

5. LinkedIn

Good for:
- Professional networking
- Special interest groups
- Collecting recommendations from previous clients
- Keeping your CV up to date
- Researching clients and contacts

Not so good for:
- Personal chit chat
- Making new connections
- Pictures of kittens

In this chapter we're looking at

- What works and what doesn't on LinkedIn
- How to fill out your LinkedIn profile
- Do you need LinkedIn Premium?

LinkedIn is a well-established site used for professional networking, and is by some margin the most sober of all the social media networks. You won't find many gratuitous pictures of cats here. I think you would have to look for a long time to find anyone who actively loves LinkedIn in the way that people love Twitter or Tumblr, and even then they probably wouldn't be a writer.

Writers aren't the best fit with LinkedIn - possibly that has something to do with the sobriety. Remember when we said Twitter was like a big pub? LinkedIn is more like a dentist's waiting room - necessary to be there, but substantially less fun.

Launched over a decade ago, it's grown enormously in recent years. In June 2013 LinkedIn had almost 260 million users in over 200 countries. It stands to reason that some of them are going to want to hire you, or at least read your writing. And that sobriety is what a lot of people like about LinkedIn - there is none of the distracting flim flam that may clutter up your other social networks. Nobody's linking to the latest list on Buzzfeed or uploading 40 pictures of their dog. This is a good thing when you're on a writing deadline.

Whilst LinkedIn was originally mainly for people in suits, these days plenty of creative types are on there, and are being offered work on there. And that's the other good thing about it - other writers are getting work via LinkedIn, and so could you. And here's a tip for newbies at the online footprint game - If you don't have a website, filling in your LinkedIn profile is a way to ensure that your details will show up high on a Google search of your name.

Recruiters do use LinkedIn to search for writers (especially copywriters, bloggers and social media consultants), so make sure your profile contains keywords that you'd like to be found under. Use your most professional-sounding email as contact (not Hotmail, that's for backpacking students on a gap year and looks a bit old-fashioned for adults).

Add updates once or twice a week but again keep them sober - no links to quizzes which tell you which Game of Thrones house you should be in. As this is very much about professional networking you can keep your updates to things which promote you. I don't link to every blog post I publish, but I will link to any posts that have a wider professional relevance.

As with any network, keep your updates focused on what your audience might be interested in hearing as opposed to what you are interested in saying. Whilst you can promote, it's best to do it in a way that's valuable to the reader.

Social media as writers use it:

Chloe Hall @chloeditorial
Copywriter and social media consultant Chloe Hall prioritised LinkedIn along with Twitter early in her writing career, moving on to use Facebook and Pinterest for her blog. She says that LinkedIn can be a fantastic tool for showcasing what you can do, as long as your profile is up to date and well laid out: "From voluntary work to examples of published work, it's been great for me to announce things as they happen, like my nomination in The Guardian's Rising Star Awards for my social media marketing efforts. This will then bring a stream of people to my profile – new connections, friends, old colleagues and the odd lurker of course! LinkedIn is an opportunity to sell yourself in a very constructed and 'safe' environment which I think attracts a lot of users who find the idea of a hard sell quite hideous.

"For writers looking for work it's a fantastic tool to put names to faces should you be looking to approach a marketing agency for example as a copywriter, or a PR agency. In terms of best practice, I always apply the same rules to my other 'professional' social media accounts and keep it informative, professional and light hearted to show I'm not a robot. I often post educational or inspiring articles I've read and the odd update of what I'm working on, or if I've been nominated for something. Self-promotion is definitely encouraged on LinkedIn, it's up to you how indulgent you are.

"I've been offered work via LinkedIn, and also unique opportunities like potentially becoming a Trustee of Newcastle Citizen's Advice Bureau. You also learn how to network 'online' by commenting on articles etc, which you can then apply to other social media profiles. Scheduling tools like Hootsuite are invaluable to me – I use them a lot with my clients, but also it is handy being able to see what's happening on Facebook, Twitter and Google Plus at the same time. 90% of my time I access social media from my iPhone as opposed to a laptop or ipad so the optimised apps are very handy."

Chloe's advice to newbies is to be yourself, and be patient "Rome wasn't built in a day and a strong social media following certainly won't. Make a list of maybe 3 or 4 people in a similar industry to you who you aspire to be like on social media. Take note of their tone of voice, content they post and who they follow and who follows them back. It's important to develop your own brand and voice on social media by engaging with people and businesses and hashtag hours [organised chats grouped around the same hashtag] for example, but it's always good to see what other people are doing and why."

How to fill out your LinkedIn profile

Think of your LinkedIn profile as being like a really comprehensive, dynamic CV. For most media jobs, it's better if your regular CV just contains brief highlights, whereas on LinkedIn you can colour in the corners as well.

Pick a fairly business-like profile pic, as that's more appropriate for this network. No pets, children or unclothed limbs here. You don't have to wear a tie; you just don't want to look like someone who works in the same clothes that they sleep in (even if you do).

The top panel of the LinkedIn profile is the space to give an overview of your career, before you get to the specifics of individual jobs and education below. It shouldn't need saying, but if you're presenting yourself as a writer then you need to write this bit well. Still sober though - keep personal flourishes to a minimum. Stick to the facts - the work you've done, the stuff you've had published. Use keywords in this section for whatever you want searchers to find you for. Repeat those keywords in the other profile sections when listing your work.

The job description that appears under your name can be up to 120 characters, so think carefully about what you put here. How are you choosing to represent yourself? This is a hard one for me because I am a typical freelance portfolio worker who does a couple of different things, but I think that's OK because it distinguishes me from a lot of other people.

The Summary section of your profile is where you set out your stall of what you have to offer, experience and skills-wise. The Experience section below that is more like a traditional CV where you list the jobs you've done.

Neither section needs to include every job you've ever had. In your summary, present the highlights of who you are and what's so great about the services you have to offer. Yes you will feel a total dweeb when writing this, so take your time and know that we've all felt your pain.

And don't forget to come back and revise these sections regularly, especially when you have something new and great to add. Filling in the LinkedIn profile can be such an almighty bore that when we've done it once, we don't want to do it again. But, like the dentist, regular visits every six months are advised.

If you don't have a lot of writing experience and are struggling with what to put, just expand a little more on the experience you do have, and add in any jobs from the rest of your working life which add to your writing life.

LinkedIn profiles are quite long and can take a while to complete, but once you've done it then it's simply a matter of tweaking and updating as your career progresses. Think about what sort of work you would like to be found for, and make sure you include those keywords in your profile. The shortcut way to do this is to look at the profile of someone who is further along in their career than you, and learn from that. You don't have to reinvent the wheel every time. Though be warned that LinkedIn does tell people who's looked at their profile so log out if you don't want to be found. You can also change the privacy settings in your LinkedIn account so that other people won't be notified that you've looked at their profile.

Ask people you've worked with to fill out a recommendation (you can do the same for them) and it turns your profile page into a CV that really packs a punch. These recommendations carry a lot of weight because they can only be solicited via LinkedIn and you can't edit them at all. So be selective and ask for them from people who know and like your work, because they've worked with you in some capacity. It's not the place to ask your friends and family to say how great you are.

You can change the URL of your LinkedIn page, but do this as soon as you can in the process and definitely before you start telling people about it or putting it on your business card (if you are the sort of writer who's going to be getting work out of LinkedIn you will need to be doing face to face networking too, and you will definitely need business cards).

The skills section of your profile

You can add in up to 200 skill sections, but you really don't need that many. Some of these sections are generated by others so you don't have that much control over what goes here. Your network can endorse your skills, and will be invited to when they log in. The actual endorsements don't really have that much weight because people sprinkle them around like confetti and don't need specific knowledge of your skills to endorse them. But over time they build up an interesting picture, so for example if you are marketing yourself as an online writer and many people have recommended your blogging, SEO and fact-checking skills, it all helps. To encourage people to endorse you, either ask them directly or start endorsing them generously. I try never to endorse somebody if I don't at least have some knowledge of their work. I might not have commissioned them, but if I've read their stuff and liked it, I'll give them a tip of the hat for editorial skills.

LinkedIn profiles are designed to be for individuals rather than businesses, so create a profile under your own name and possibly a separate page for your business if you think it merits it. If you have a pen name, you can always have two separate accounts for your writing name and your real name, but then again this becomes one more thing to administrate. Personally I think it's better to have one account under the name you want to be found by; the name you want people to hire you under or buy your books.

LinkedIn is probably of least use to fiction authors, and of most use to copywriters, online writers and social media consultants. Unless you choose to really dig deep and get involved with the groups, for most of us LinkedIn will be a once a month update. Look for people you might like to be connected with and send out invitations to connect. Think of it as a way to strengthen the connections you've made elsewhere. So if you recognise a name because you've chatted on Twitter or you're in the same Facebook group, then go ahead and invite them to connect. Don't take it personally if they don't accept your request though. Lots of people don't look at those notifications or respond to them particularly quickly. Many people only go on to LinkedIn when they're actively seeking work. Yes I know for us freelancers that means all the time, but believe it or not for some people it's not that often.

And don't pass by the Honors and Awards section - have you got something to put in there? Even if it's just a blog award that you nominated yourself for, it all counts. No, it doesn't count as much as a Pulitzer but it still counts. It's still a thing that you achieved so take the credit.

You've created your profile - what next?
Once you're happy with your LinkedIn profile, you can start to tell people about it. The site also creates code for you to make a

badge linking to your profile to put on your website.

The settings allow you to control your privacy and decide who you want to see your profile - ranging from everybody on the internet to you and you alone. Since you are here for professional purposes and want people to find and hire you, keep your privacy settings as open as possible. The only time you might not want to do that is if you are in the middle of reworking your profile and you aren't quite ready for people to see it yet.

LinkedIn sometimes changes what you can do on its profiles and doesn't exactly advertise the fact, so keep your ears and eyes open for any changes to ensure you are always making the most of the system.

Ask to connect with other people - the site itself will suggest who, plus you can go and seek out colleagues and professional connections. LinkedIn was originally set up to extend connections with people who already knew each other, but that's much more loosely applied nowadays, and it is fine to ask to connect with someone you don't know but could have a legitimate interest in.

Other ways to use LinkedIn
Once you've filled in the profile, it's not simply a case of sitting back and waiting for work to come to you. You can also search for LinkedIn profiles of people you're intending to work with, to check them out. Let's say you're speaking with an editor or a new client about potential work - you could check out their LinkedIn profile to see where they've worked before and get a feel for what they might be looking for. The world of media is not that big the more you dig into it, so chances are you might

know someone they know, which all helps to cement relationships. Of course this is slightly drifting into the acceptable face of stalking, so remember to search incognito when you're looking up their profile if you don't want them to know that you've looked.

And of course don't forget ye olde job search on LinkedIn. Lots and lots of companies advertise their vacancies on LinkedIn, and you can search via job title, company, location or any of the above.

Organising your network on LinkedIn
Just as other social networks will allow you to group your connections, so LinkedIn will let you do this via what it calls Tags - it's the LinkedIn version of lists on Twitter or circles on Google Plus. It's a useful thing to do if you've built up a big network which is a hodge-podge of people you'd like to keep in touch with and those you're not sure why they're there.

You can tag a group of contacts and then send an email via LinkedIn to up to 50 of them at once. Be very careful if you do this so you don't fall into the trap of spamming. Save it for major announcements like a new book, and even then think twice.

Joining groups
There are many groups for writers on LinkedIn, but most of them seem to be filled with people in search of their first writing job, and no one looking to hire. I think these are of limited use. But groups can be great if you have a professional niche and are looking to find more people in that niche too - say, if you're a business writer then you might want to join

groups relevant to your specialist niche. If you write web copy for a particular type of company then seek out groups relevant to them.

If you join a group, commit to it for the long haul and don't just drop a spammy link to your website then run. When you're updating your profile every six months or so, evaluate which groups are proving to be a good investment of your time and which you need to quietly back away from.

Running LinkedIn pages for clients

This is kind of tricky to navigate, since it's not what LinkedIn wants at all. It wants individual profiles to be run by individuals, not you ghostwriting a client's profile for them. It is doable, and I've done it professionally, but it is clunky and not straightforward at all. To incorporate LinkedIn into your social media offering, you need to be very familiar with all aspects of creating a great profile, plus creating and running a great company page.

LinkedIn Premium

Like all services that offer up some of the goodies for free, what LinkedIn really wants is for you to pay for its services. To tempt you to do this, it will offer you a month's trial of its premium service for free. By all means try it out, but only do it in a month when you're not overloaded with work and can give it the attention to really explore.

Extra benefits of Premium include:

- The ability to message someone you're not already connected to

- See more profiles when you search
- See exactly who has viewed your profile, and the keywords that brought them there - on the free version you can see a few, not the full stalkers' line up
- See full profiles of people outside your network

I think that with most services you know when you've reached the edge of what the free service can give you and when you want to do more, so much so that you will pay for it. Until that happens, LinkedIn free is probably enough for most of us.

And if you find you've enjoyed posting extended updates on LinkedIn, perhaps you're ready to start your own blog?

6. Your website and blog

Good for:
- Providing a showcase for your work and marketing you online 24/7
- Making it easier for editors and other contacts to get in touch
- Learning new skills that will support your paid work as an online writer
- Successful blogs can become a source of income in themselves

Not so good for:
- Becoming an enormous time suck that takes focus away from other writing projects
- Getting you too used to working without an editor

In this chapter we're looking at:
- Why you need a website, and why you may or may not benefit from a blog too
- Easy ways to build your site and blog
- How to find images for your blog posts
- What to do to attract traffic to your blog
- How to promote your books with a blog tour
- How to make money from your blog
- Writing blog posts professionally for clients

If you've come to this chapter wondering whether you need a website, then the answer is yes, yes you most certainly do. We're in an era now where professional writers have websites to show potential readers and clients who they are and what they can do. It's as simple as that. Your local cafe and your twelve-year-old nephew probably have websites, as do the generation of writers coming up behind you - are you any less professional than them?

Your website doesn't have to be a complicated affair, but it should contain some personal background about you, a recentish photo, contact details and examples of previously published work. You could also link to your social media channels - your Twitter account, G+ profile and Facebook page. Link to any of your work that's been published online and to your books on Amazon.

If you are just starting out as a writer then it can be daunting to do this, as you may feel that you haven't got much to show so far. But everybody's got to start somewhere and if anything, it's probably easier if you've got less to put in rather than too much to choose from. You can include anything you've written for free, especially if the site you wrote for looks professional enough. As time goes on and you get more published in better titles you can replace that stuff.

I've got a couple of different websites - one that promotes my media career coaching, and another one that promotes me as a freelance journalist and author. Then I've got my blog, Opposable Thumbs, which acts as a bridge between the two. Probably the most important page within all of this is the *Samples of Previously Published Work* page on my journalism site, which I send when I'm pitching to a new editor. I keep this page up to date by linking to anything new that's been published, adding in scans of offline stuff and weeding out the older stuff as necessary. It doesn't show everything I've ever written, but it contains a representative sample of my experience.

Website = Yes; Blog = Maybe

A blog is not as compulsory as a website, but it can be a lot of fun and good for your writing at the same time. It does involve a time commitment, but if you find other forms of social media such as Twitter or Facebook a bit too bite sized and fast paced then your energies might be better placed on a blog. If, on the other hand, you are pushed for time then Twitter is an easier entry into the world of social media than a blog.

Only start a blog if you can commit to updating it regularly. Every second of every day, two more new blogs are created. There are millions and millions already in existence - some abandoned, others thriving. But there is still a place for your unique voice.

The great gift that blogging gives to writers is that it helps you to become a better writer. Not that you can't become a better writer without a blog; it's just that if you do start blogging, it won't be time wasted. It will help you come up with not just one idea, but many. It will be a place for you to try out those ideas and see how they play before you turn them into something more. It can be your own personal soapbox, a place to say things that you think need to be said without having to go via an editor - of course, this is not always a good thing, but it can be pretty refreshing and liberating. Your blogging could easily get you spotted for paid writing or other opportunities. But before we get to the blog, let's start with the site. Your blog, if you start one, can live on your website, or elsewhere.

Designing your website (and blog if you want one)

You don't need a fancy schmancy expensive website. You could easily build one yourself, or get a schoolkid to do it for you. It doesn't have to cost a lot of money (though you can pay a lot if you're that way inclined). You could do it yourself for almost free, even with virtually non-existent tech skills. If you have a single website for you and your writing, you probably won't need separate sites for any future books or projects you may undertake.

All website building and blogging platforms have pre-set, free themes/designs available to use. In general, the less you know about website design, the simpler your design needs to be. The Mr Site package is also very popular amongst writers as it's an inexpensive, DIY website building tool.

The big advantage to building it yourself is that although it may be a steep learning curve, you will be acquiring great skills and are in a prime position to develop your site yourself in the future. When you hire someone to do all that stuff, you may start off with a great looking site, but what happens when you want to change or add something?

If you do get someone to build it for you, at the very least find out how to add widgets to it. Widgets are little bits of code that do things like add in your Twitter stream or link to your Facebook page. All the bits and bobs that you see in the side margins of blogs - those were created via widgets. Adding them is usually a very easy cut and paste job, once you know what to cut and where to paste. Don't be scared; it's very simple to do. If you can make toast, you can do this. That's the level of technical ability we're talking about.

To create a free site, I recommend using Wordpress.com. There is also Blogger, but I recommend Wordpress because more professional publishers use it and therefore knowing your way round a Wordpress dashboard is a marketable skill for a 21st century writer to have.

However, if you intend to make money directly via your site by selling adverts then Wordpress.com doesn't allow this (it keeps the service free by adding its own adverts). They have recently changed rules so that you can earn money via sponsored posts (advertorials) on wordpress.com but you still can't sell advertising from third parties. Therefore if you're intending on creating a commercial site, you'll need to do it via Wordpress.org, which can do more and has low ongoing running costs. Both versions of Wordpress take a bit of getting to grips with initially, but it's not difficult. They have very good user support forums which will be able to help when you get stuck.

If you're setting up a site, you'll probably want your own domain name, so your site address is yourname.com, rather than yourname.wordpress.com (as it would be if you simply kept the free site version). A domain name is not expensive - often under £10 / $15 per year. If your name is already registered by somebody else, like Twitter you need to find a variation that works for you, like JoeBloggsBooks.com or JoeBloggsWriting.com

What to include in your website
It's essential to include multiple options of easy contact details that will reach you quickly. Media may want to contact you for expert quotes, or editors may want to call you for short deadline assignments, so there's no point in giving a phone

number that you never answer or an email address that you only check once a week. Don't use a contact form - a direct email address or phone number is much more likely to be used. If you're nervous about publishing those details too openly you can always set up a gmail address that's just for the site, and have it redirect to your main email.

Link to any published works. Sign up for an Amazon Affiliates account to create thumbnail links directly to your books in its store. A reader who likes your site can then click through to buy your books. And as an affiliate you will make 5% of whatever they buy when they click through your link. If they click through and purchase a big haul, you're quids in. In addition, you'll also make your regular royalties on the books you sell. See, this website is paying for itself already. From time to time, check that your published writing links actually work, and that any online work you've done hasn't been moved or deleted.

Plan to update your site regularly. Obviously if you are a novelist who only publishes one book every year or two then your website won't need to be updated so often, though you may want to add in news of talks and signings etc. But if you are a journalist with regular new articles being published, these need to be added to your site.

Social media as writers use it:

Dane Cobain @danecobain
Writer Dane Cobain runs the book blog SocialBookshelves.com and wouldn't be without social media "Facebook and Twitter are both invaluable, most of the writers that I know use both of them.

Personally, I also like to use YouTube, although I mainly use that for my book blog, and Instagram is great for accentuating any imagery that you have. I also love Goodreads – it's a great way for authors and readers to connect.

"From my book blog in particular, I've got to attend a lot of events and received a lot of freebies that I wouldn't normally get. It's great to go to events, such as book launches etc., because you get to schmooze with publishers and writers and just generally be a part of the writing scene. Most of the opportunities that I've had through my book blog have taken me to places that my writing alone might not have.

"TweetDeck is a godsend if you manage multiple Twitter accounts like I do (around a dozen at the moment). Otherwise, there's nothing particularly special that I use – just separate tools here and there that do different things. TweetReach, for example, will give you an indication of how many people saw your tweets in a given period, while ManageFlitter helps you to organise who you're following."

Dane advises newbies to go for it without hesitation (or alcohol) "Just jump straight in and embrace it – at the end of the day, it's another medium in which to express yourself, and so you should jump at the chance. There's no real right or wrong when it comes to representing yourself – my one piece of advice would be not to post anything while drunk, and not to post anything that you wouldn't want your grandmother to read."

Blogging - for yourself and for others

You have to put the effort in to run a good blog - time both in actually writing the posts, but also in sourcing images and telling people about your blog so they can come read it. But whilst it's time-consuming, it's also one of the most fun outlets.

What you blog about, and how often, is entirely up to you. You might choose to start each day with a quick blog post, or you could stick to once a month news roundups telling your readers what you've been up to.

Depending on what kind of writer you are, your work may or may not provide blog fodder. If you're a feature writer who's out and about several times a week seeing and doing interesting things, then you're probably set for umpteen blog posts. If you're in your house writing a novel then it's harder because the main focus of your life will be what you're creating on a day to day basis.

If that's the case, your blog may serve you better if it focuses on another area of your life - something you like to do, or something you're passionate about. Right now, as my main daily time is spent writing this book and I only really leave the house when pushed, my blog is full of reviews of whatever home shopping craze I've been procrastinating with.

A long term blog changes over time, as your life changes. You don't have to wear your heart on your sleeve when you're blogging. Some people are happy to blog about very personal issues such as mental or physical health, but that doesn't mean it's compulsory to give away more than you are comfortable with. There can be a lot to gain from sharing your inner life with a wider community, but equally it can serve you well to keep something back. At least until an editor is paying you.

With promoting your books on your blog, obviously you can be more direct and reference them more often, as it's your space. But don't go over the top about it, since regular readers of your blog will know that you write books already. Find ways to build natural references to your books into your blog - perhaps there's a current news story that references your book. Think about how the topics and themes of your writing connect to current news - latest surveys and events; the time of year or anniversaries. If you write fiction, there will still be a connection between your work and the real world which could make a great blog post. It doesn't need to be a deep and epic revelation - a typical blog post can be as short as 300 words. If you find yourself motoring past 800 words then think about splitting it into more than one post.

When my book about fear of driving was coming out, I referenced it in a number of ways on my blog. First of all, there were the posts about my own fear of driving before I had even got as far as writing a book. Then there was the excited update when I finally got a publishing contract. From time to time I'd add a post if I was looking for something in particular (like case studies for the book). And obviously the date of publication had to be announced. Once the book had been out for a while and I was getting feedback from readers about the bits they found most useful, this became a 'Top Tips' style post. From time to time I get approached by TV companies researching the subject, so I'll write a post inviting people with driving phobia to get in touch with them. I've also asked other driving experts to write guest posts for me. All of this is spread across around three years, interspersed with posts about many other subjects, so although it looks a lot when you gather it together, it wouldn't be overwhelming for the casual reader who isn't interested in that subject.

The great thing about blog readers is that they are often amongst your most engaged fans. So not only will they buy your books (and you'll see that they do when you check your Amazon Affiliates account), they will recommend them to others as well. That's the kind of fans you want.

Blog posts - like writing, but different

The big difference between running your own blog and other forms of writing is that you're in charge of everything - there's no editor or publisher to pitch to; it's down to you to spot your own typos. Publishing becomes a button you press rather than a long term process. It's a great way for potential readers, clients and others to get to know you and how you write in a more immediate way.

The down side is that all this power can be intoxicating - when you've spent time in a kingdom that you rule it can be hard to dance to somebody else's tune, and follow somebody else's style sheet.

And it's not enough to simply blog and assume people will find it. You will need to get out there and blow your own trumpet so that people will come and read your posts. So at a minimum you'll need to be on Twitter to attract readers, and Google Plus and Facebook will help too.

I've been writing my blog Opposable Thumbs for over seven years and the content has varied a lot in that time. Right now I'm calling it 'Geeky Lifestyle' in an attempt to make it slightly more unified. The current advice for commercial blogs says that you need to have a theme or a niche, so that readers know what to expect. If you're not so bothered about your blog being purely commercial then a defined niche is less vital, and you

...u turn it into a kind of magazine about the things you're interested in.

Whilst the subject matter has changed, the one thing that has always been consistent in my blog is the tone of voice, and that's also consistent with my books - warm, practical, down to earth. That's my thing. So through the blog, you know what you're going to get in the books.

Any blog post you write could be read by someone who will hire you to write for them, or buy one of your books. With that in mind, keep your standards high, and consistently high. As with any other form of social media, if you show up with garbled grammar and too many typos then people will assume that you always write like that.

You set your own blogging schedule. Right now I prefer longer posts once or twice a week, that I can really put some effort into creating and promoting, but some weeks there is more than that to say. In the first month of your blog's life it's a good idea to post as often as you can to get plenty of content in there, but after that you can ease off a bit if you like.

Blog posts don't have to be long - the Google search engine likes them to be at least 400 words as it equates longer with better, but if you have a few decent pictures or a video then you could get away with less than that.

Think about the keyword before you write a post - in essence, what is this post about? What sums it up? What would people be likely to type into Google to find this post? Writing a post with the aim of it being easily found online is called Search Engine Optimisation, and you will often see job ads for online writers asking for SEO skills. The best way to demonstrate that you have those skills is by using them writing posts that do well in search engines. SEO is a very organic subject in that it's changing and developing every day. It's a bit of a slippery fish - just when you think you've got a good grasp of it, it shoots off in a new direction. There's always something new to learn about SEO, which is what I find fascinating about it. Social Media Examiner is a good site if you want to read more on this. http://www.socialmediaexaminer.com/

Images for your blog posts
Even though you're a wordsmith, every blog post you write will need a unique image. Yes I know this is the job of a picture editor, but increasingly online writers are being asked to supply images too, so you might as well get in the habit of doing so. Like SEO and knowing your way round Wordpress, it's an essential skill for a 21st century professional writer. For blogs today, images are not optional - each post needs a unique image of its own so that when people share it on Facebook or wherever, the site has something to pick up as a thumbnail image.

Obviously for copyright reasons you can't just rip images off the internet for your blog. So where to find them? Here are five places to find free and legal images to use on your blog. I prefer to create my own images, but if that's not possible then I nearly always go to Flickr Creative Commons.

- **Create your own images**
  This should always be your first choice, as it will make your blog more unique if you use pictures that you've created. You don't need an expensive camera – most smartphone cameras are up to the job. Use sites and

apps such as PicMonkey, Instagram, Instacollage or Pixlr to improve your image, create collages or add effects and words. Have fun and be creative when you're illustrating your posts.

- **Flickr Creative Commons**

  These photographers are happy for you to use their work as long as you credit them and link back to the source. Try sorting your image search under 'Interesting' (look for the sorting tag in the top left hand side).

- **Morguefile**

  Yes this free photo archive has got a gruesome name but if you are inclined to be a bit emo then that's probably a bonus. You can use this site to find great, free photos or browse the information to pick up tips about how to become a better photographer yourself.

- **Stock.Xchng**

  You have to register to use this site, but once you do you'll have a choice of many thousands of free stock images to use. Try not to use the first ones your search throws up, because that's the obvious choice. You can still be unexpected even if it's not your own original image.

- **Getty Images**

  Getty recently introduced an embed tool to allow bloggers access to its 35 million photo archive. When you use the tool, the photo will already have a credit to Getty and a link back to its' licensing page. Getty is a good choice if you want current news or sports images.

So you've written a blog post - what next?

It's not enough to write the post and expect it to be an instant viral hit with the masses. You need to let people know that your post exists so they will be able to read it if they want to. And this is where your other social media platforms come into play.

You could

- Link to your blog post on Facebook
  Either on your personal feed or author page or both, or in appropriate groups if it's relevant
- Tweet about your new blog post
  You can do this more than once, but make sure you leave at least three hours between tweets so different sets of eyeballs will see it. Vary your wording to see what makes people click more. Use a scheduling tool like Hootsuite or Buffer to set up a few tweets about your blog post.
- Pin the picture to Pinterest
- Link to your post on Google +

Don't post to all these platforms at once. The people who know you on Facebook may well be following you on Twitter and possibly on G+ too, and it will be very boring and off-putting for them to see the same link popping up from you again and again.

When I publish a blog post, I generally tweet and G+ a link as soon as it's published, then tweet it again a few times over the next week.

The next day I might link to Pinterest, Facebook and any groups or sites I think it's relevant to. Each of these actions takes seconds. Posting to G+ means that Google will instantly know about your link, rather than waiting for its own programs to find it, and this will help you attract more traffic. With any of these platforms, if you post a link, stick around or check back in soon in case there are any comments from readers.

Connecting with other blogs and blogging communities

It's important to realise that blogging is a community activity, and as such the best way to attract readers to your blog is by reading and commenting on other people's blogs. Join groups to connect with other like-minded bloggers, find other blogs to comment on, and attend blogger meet ups in your area.

This is where blogging can start to become more of a time suck because honestly, there are a gazillion blogging groups out there, especially on Facebook. Don't feel you have to join every one - it's not Pokemon, you haven't gotta catch 'em all. If you're starting to feel like you're in too many networks then you probably are.

Don't assume that just because you are a professional writer that you are somehow a more evolved being than the hobbyists in blogging groups. This is a mistake I've seen many writers make, especially journalists who take up blogging but retain a slightly sniffy attitude towards other bloggers. As they said in High School Musical, we're all in this together. Your fellow bloggers are your team on your blogging adventure - you'll get much further with them supporting you than you would on your own. Those people are your supporters, your army, your friends. And right now they probably know way more about blogging than you do.

As a side benefit - if you're a freelance journalist looking for case studies then blogging groups are a great place to frequent as you will meet people from a very wide range of backgrounds who are usually not shy in coming forward. Once they get to know you as a blogger they will be more likely to trust you as a journalist. Bloggers can also be very helpful when it comes to publicising your book, so make some copies available to send out.

Promoting your books with a blog tour
This is like a regular book tour, except you don't have to leave your house, which may or may not be a good thing. How it works is that you arrange to 'appear' on a bunch of blogs every day, via an interview, guest post or giveaway.

I promoted my first book Toddlers: An Instruction Manual via guest posting on over 20 blogs. To set it up, I simply went into a number of Facebook parenting blog groups I belong to and asked who would like a unique guest post from me. In return I asked that the bloggers linked to my book on Amazon. Doing it this way meant that I didn't waste time emailing bloggers who might not be interested - instead I asked people to raise their hands, and then proceeded with those who did.

For the actual guest posts I took short extracts (around 250-400 words) from the book and reworked them slightly so that they'd read well as a blog post. This meant that I didn't have to write a bunch of new stuff. When I sent the guest posts in, I also included a jpeg of the book cover and many of the bloggers were happy to include this with the post.

Guest posting like this can be a great way to get your writing in front of an audience that would not otherwise have heard of you. And then it stays online for as long as the blog does (hopefully forever), so it's marketing that goes on working. If you are looking to place guest posts to promote your writing, think carefully and only do it on blogs who have an audience that is likely to be interested in your book.

Popular bloggers get asked to place guest posts a lot, and many charge for this because they know that space on their blog has worth. But most won't charge if they know and trust you as a fellow blogger. You wouldn't get that in a magazine.

Blog giveaways

Giving away your books (or somebody else's) can be a great way to raise traffic for your site. Everybody loves a freebie. The danger with relying on giveaways too much, however, is that this traffic tends not to be sticky - people buzz in to try and win something but then don't stick around for anything else. If you are short on supplies of your book I wouldn't rush to offer them as a giveaway prize - probably better to give them to someone who is definitely going to review the book.

If you have an active blog then you may find companies occasionally offer you prizes to give away and these are worth considering. It still takes time to create and promote a contest so don't say yes to all. But if you are developing a commercial blog then giveaways can be a good way to bump up your traffic, which looks good to advertisers.

I occasionally run giveaways on my sites but I only agree to do them if it's an attractive, potentially popular prize - maybe something of high value or from a high profile brand. People can enter by subscribing to the blog or following me on Twitter or liking my Facebook page. So I get increased traffic and subscribers and somebody gets a nice prize. It's a win-win really - the best type of win of all.

Tracking your blog statistics

Tracking who's reading your blog, where they come from and what pages they stop at is an interesting and useful thing to do. The actual numbers don't matter as much as the fact that it's all increasing. You'll get an insight into which posts gain most readers and what to do more of.

If you really get into blogging, especially if you decide to run a commercial blog, then it's worthwhile installing Google Analytics so you can analyse your blog traffic and where it's coming from in more detail. Otherwise, the Wordpress dashboard will show you basic stats of how many hits your blog is getting each day and where in the world they're coming from. Google Analytics can't be backdated so it's worth installing at the start if you think you might want that kind of information in the future.

Comments on your blog

Always reply to any comments left on your blog (apart from the spammers, you can delete them). People who've done you the courtesy of leaving a comment deserve an acknowledgement of this, and if they've left a link to their blog it's a nice touch to pop over there and leave a comment too. Most commenting systems require the commenter to leave their email address, but this does not mean that you have permission to harvest those addresses and use them for any further marketing purposes.

Don't be disheartened if you don't get many comments - many bloggers report that the number of comments has decreased in recent years. This is largely put down to the fact that a lot of people read blog posts on their phones and it's much harder to comment from there. All the more reason to cherish the people who do comment.

Social media as writers use it:

Patricia Carswell @pcarswell

Journalist, copywriter and award-winning blogger Patricia Carswell originally took up blogging to showcase her writing, but found that the benefits turned out to be much greater: "I have used Twitter and Facebook to great effect as a journalist to find out information and search for case studies, as well as for networking, and my rowing blog www.GirlOnTheRiver.com has led directly to several commissions. Two profitable copywriting clients came to me as the directors had read and enjoyed the blog and wanted me to liven up some copy using the same tone. My blog has also led directly to commissions from a rowing magazine and through that I gained membership of the British Association of Rowing Journalists. And I have become sufficiently adept at social media that I have been paid by several clients to run their social media accounts for them.

"My advice to anyone blogging to promote their work is to balance being yourself with being professional. A blog certainly doesn't need to be written in a formal style, and it's important for the tone and style to be authentic, but it's worth paying attention to your grammar and spelling and to make it look reasonably well-designed.

"If you have clients in mind, and you feature personally in your blog, you might want to think carefully about what photographs you use on the blog and in your associated social media. I don't mind clients seeing pictures of me in lycra, looking tired and sweaty after a race, but I'm careful not to post anything that would be embarrassing in a business meeting with a corporate client.

Patricia reassures newbies that you'll soon get the hang of it "Most people learn by trial and error, and the great thing about being new to social media is that you don't have many followers so your mistakes aren't seen by many people! Having said that, a blog does need a bit more planning. It's worth reading advice on starting blogs as there are plenty of rookie mistakes that you can easily avoid. There are plenty of blogging networks online, where you can ask for advice and pick up lots of useful tips. A well-planned blog with a few posts already ready to go and a decent design is more likely to pick up followers and be trusted by brands and potential clients.

"It's also worth remembering that being a great writer doesn't necessarily make you a great blogger. The blogging world is informal and beautiful writing isn't always valued as much as you might expect or like. Lifestyle blogs are often glorified photo albums and your photography and design skills will be more important than your ability to write. Venturing into that world can be quite humbling for someone who has confined themselves to traditional writing."

Writing commercial blog posts

Once you have some blogging experience, you're then in a good position to take on commercial blogging work, either as a one off or on an ongoing basis running a blog for a company. If you're a copywriter then you may find you'll get offered work like this by companies for whom you already write web copy.

Just as a few years ago companies woke up to the fact that they needed a website, now they're waking up to the fact that that's not enough, so to have more of a new media conversation that means a blog and maybe a Twitter feed and Facebook page too. So who better to ask than the person who's already doing your online writing work? This is why a blog is useful for a copywriter - you might not be promoting your work in the way a novelist or a journalist would, but you are acquiring professional blogging skills that you can then offer to clients

And what to charge for this sort of work? For rates always think in terms of time rather than per word, and whatever your day rate might be for copywriting. So it very much depends on what sort of blog post you're being asked to write - is it a minimal research 500 words that you could easily write in an hour? Or will it involve more in depth research and interviews? Is it a one off or a regular contract generating new posts every week? Find out as much as you can so you can estimate how much time it might take and work out a quote accordingly.

Social media as writers use it:

Jane Common @JaneCommon
Jane Common was an established freelance journalist when she took up blogging at www.PhileasDogg.com to document her travels with her dog, Attlee. This led directly to a book deal, with some unexpected personal benefits for Jane "I started my blog <u>PhileasDogg</u> because, finding myself 40, single and struck down with a bout of depression my therapist suggested doing something for half an hour a day that would take me out of myself. I'd been thinking, for a few months, of writing a travel blog from my dog Attlee's point of view.

"Around the same time I read an article in a magazine and one of the messages it contained resonated with me. If you have an idea, it said, stick with it. Most ideas fail because people give up on them too quickly so, the next halfway decent idea that strikes, persevere with it.

I began Phileas Dogg with that in mind. Writing it was easy – Attlee's charismatic and has a strong personality so finding his voice didn't prove a challenge. And 'being Attlee' as I wrote was good for me. Whenever I'm down, Attlee lifts my spirits and, for a perennial self-doubter like me, seeing the confidence with which he faces the world is uplifting. So spending an hour in his mind was therapeutic. For a short period I wasn't depressed Jane – I was my cheerful and upbeat little dog!

The blog, initially a basic build and block design which I rather clunkily constructed, dawdled along for its first four months but praise from friends and the odd email from a stranger enquiring about our travels (always addressed to Attlee) kept me going.

Then, in January 2012, a friend offered to re-design it for me. He did a wonderful job and Attlee suddenly had a really professional looking outfit on his paws.

When the website had been up and running for about nine months I contacted an agent who specialised in non-fiction. A couple of people had suggested I should try to turn the blog into a book and I was feeling stronger now – I had a focus outside work and was meeting new people through Phileas Dogg. The agent was interested in a vague sort of way and suggested I write a sample chapter, which I duly did. Afterwards, he remained interested, but still only in a vague sort of way. The idea of the blog becoming a book stalled.

I carried on blogging. A journalist from Waitrose Weekend magazine featured the website in an article; various local papers interviewed Attlee and I when we visited their neighbourhood and then, the piece de resistance, The Guardian advised its readers: 'Even if you're not a dog-owner, we urge you to read this site'. Editors I approached liked the fact that the blog was different, in that it was written by Attlee, and that we had a fair-sized mailing list and Facebook and Twitter following. In May 2013 I signed a contract and Phileas Dogg THE BOOK became a reality.

And, at last, in April 2014, a parcel arrived at my door containing copies of Phileas Dogg's Guide to Dog-Friendly Holidays in Britain. I wept with pride. We – Attlee and I – had done it. We'd written a book! It feels like an amazing achievement and I'm just so grateful to my little Battersea scruff for giving me the inspiration and confidence to go for it."

How I make money via my blog

Whether your blog leads to a book deal or not, blogging is a very legitimate worldwide profession these days. A small number of people make their living solely from blogging, but for most of us it's more likely to be part of our freelance writing mix.

These are all ways my blog has added to my income in the last year:

- **Direct writing commissions**

  Somebody read my blog, liked how I write and asked me to write for their site. To attract commissions like this, it's important to make it clear on your site that you are a professional writer, since otherwise you will get a lot of people inviting you to contribute to their sites for free. I still get those, but I ignore them.

- **Book royalties**

  Somebody (several somebodies) reads about my books on my blog, clicks through and buys one, and I get the royalties

- **Affiliate commission**

  An affiliate scheme is where, if someone clicks through your link and buys something on your recommendation, you get commission. It can work well for brands that you're passionate about and would be blogging about anyway. Individually it may only be small amounts, but it all adds up and is an easy way to earn a bit more without doing any more than you were going to do anyway.

- **Sponsored posts**

  These are similar to magazine advertorial, but the sponsor is probably more interested in the link to their site than the content around it. Rates vary a lot for this, and are currently much lower in the USA than they are in the UK. Ask in any blogger groups you belong to for current information on this.

- **Getting hired for consultancy work**

  Again, someone has read what I think on the blog and has hired me to repeat it in a more formal setting, either by making a presentation, writing a document or attending a meeting. High rates and easy, interesting work make this a fun job to do, but these roles don't tend to come along all that often. It's not the sort of work you can easily apply for either - all you can do it raise your professional profile, build your social media network and hope to get noticed. But if you do those well enough, you probably will.

Other things I could do to make money on my blog include:

- **Selling advertising**
  Either one off box adverts, or via a blog advertising network (Google for these as there are several). The reason I don't do this is because I believe it would make my blog more commercial than I want it to be. There are ads on my blog for my book so people can click and buy them on Amazon, and I want those ads to stand out and not get lost in a sea of other stuff.

- **Brand associations**
  Also known as Brand Ambassadorships, these involve being closely associated with a brand in exchange for products or (more likely) a fee. Top bloggers charge many thousands for this sort of arrangement - it's the new version of celebrity endorsement. I steer clear of these because as a journalist it is hard-wired into me not to get too much into the pockets of PRs.

- **Charge for reviews**
  I don't really agree with doing this - I think it compromises the objectivity of the review, and turns it into advertorial/sponsored post. But other bloggers definitely are, so I guess if you can find a way to charge for reviews that sits well with you ethically then good luck to you.

- **Charge for hosting competitions**

  I can understand why this is becoming a chargeable service - it takes time and skills to administer a competition, and it's not always fun. At the moment I run competitions for the fun of it - the extra traffic and the warm fuzzy feeling of giving someone a cool prize.

- **Sell products**

  Books aren't the only thing you can sell via your blog. Stitched a cushion? Made a cake? Built a time machine? A blog can easily bolt on to an online shop. I was thinking of selling withering looks, because I make those on a daily basis, but the postage costs put me off.

- **Sell a course**

  Ecourses seem to be pretty popular with many bloggers as you can write the material once and sell it many times. This works well if you have a how to/solving a problem sort of blog.

- **Offer paid subscriptions to your blog on Kindle**

  Why people pay for blog subscriptions on Kindle when they could get them for free on the internet I do not know, but they do. It's a slightly fiddly but reasonably painless process to list your blog on Amazon as a paid subscription

So as you can see there is a lot of potential for a blog to become another arm of your writing business. Don't just dismiss it as writing for free. To get to the point where there are commercial benefits to your blog you will need to spend time creating content and building up an engaged audience. Your blog could be wildly successful, but that's highly unlikely to happen overnight. And this is why, great as it is, it's not for everyone. But if it interests you, try it. You might like it more than you think.

If only there was a less time consuming way to engage with readers than blogging. Well, since there's something for everyone in the social media world, it turns out that there's a way to do that too. Step this way as we take a peep at Tumblr and YouTube.

7. Tumblr & YouTube

Good for:
- Short, snappy blog and vlog (video blog) posts
- Quick creativity - an idea can become a post very fast, often faster than traditional blogging
- Showcasing your public appearances
- Pictures of Benedict Cumberbatch, and cats
- Short form blogs devoted to one particular short-lived subject
- Authors and journalists who want to reach young adults

Less good for:
- Showcasing your writing - these platforms are more about showcasing yourself, and hoping that will interest people enough to check out your writing
- Finding case studies - this is where the anonymous people hang out, and they are unlikely to want to be case studies
- Engaging with adults - both these platforms are much more popular with teens

In this chapter we're looking at
- What are Tumblr and YouTube, and how do they differ from other forms of social media?
- How you can leverage them to promote your writing
- Engaging with your audience on Tumblr & YouTube

What is Tumblr and how is it different to regular blogging?
Tumblr is a microblogging platform, meaning that it's populated by tiny blog posts, often picture-heavy and with very few words. Although it's really more of a re-blogging platform as users reblog and share posts they like which have been created by other users. Note that Tumblr etiquette is to credit the original creator of the post - reblogging involves linking to the original creator. Reposting, on the other hand, refers to taking someone's post and reposting it on your blog as if it was your own creation. Unsurprisingly, this is frowned upon.

Tumblr is for topics that don't quite have enough meat to warrant a long blog post but can inspire some fun pictures. What all this sharing means is that there is far less new stuff being written on Tumblr (hence the 'microblogging'), and it's much more visual than other types of blog platform. It's about pictures much more than words. Occasionally people write longer Tumblr posts but it's rare.

If you want to blog but don't really have the time to do so, then Tumblr is a good option for minimum effort versus reasonably snazzy output. It's fast moving, provokes instant reactions and is where all the teens who've left Facebook are currently hanging out. If you like pretty pictures and cool graphics you'll love it. It's way, way less formal than LinkedIn. Since the emphasis is less on the word and more of the image, you might assume that Tumblr has less to offer writers. However, it's a network of over 188 million blogs - over 83 billion posts - so don't discount them out of hand.

On your Tumblr dashboard, you follow other people and they might follow you. Additionally, anyone who has the URL can see what you post, so you can share this stuff via your other social media networks too. You could also connect your blogs to your Twitter and Facebook accounts, so whenever you make a post, it would also be sent as a tweet and a status update. But as we've discussed previously, think hard before doing this because the same thing does not work across all networks and you don't want to risk spamming your friends. Also, the teens of Tumblr don't tend to do this so you will look a bit like an old fuddy duddy if your Tumblr posts start popping up on Facebook.

When to update on Tumblr

How often you update your Tumblr is entirely up to you - it could be once a week or several times a day. If you already have a blog then you probably don't need a Tumblr as well, unless your writing is aimed at the Young Adult sector, or you are just writing for fun and want to share your work with others. The author John Green is an active user of Tumblr and has over 8 million subscribers on YouTube, and he's done pretty well out of it. If it's YAs you're after, then Tumblr is a must and you can probably ditch the long form blog, unless you want to reach the parents of the YAs who will actually be buying your books.

The other thing that Tumblr is useful for is for brief, short-term blogging - maybe you have a book or other tightly-focused project which you want to promote in the immediate future, but you don't anticipate running for years. A dedicated Tumblr could serve you very well. For example, the author John Higgs launched a Tumblr to mark the release of his book about art-music pioneers The KLF http://klfbook.tumblr.com/ - this contains snippets from the text paired with automatically generated images, so once the site was set up it needed very little extra input. Higgs also set up another, more traditional promotional Tumblr (inasmuch as there's anything traditional about these things) to upload stories and images relevant to the

book, which other Tumblr users then reblogged and spread around their networks:
http://thefuckersburnedthelot.tumblr.com/

If you do decide to go down the Tumblr route, you will probably need to build up a bigger network and many more followers than you would if you were blogging. With so much happening, it's harder to be memorable and stand out. But if you persist and produce good content, you could build up a loyal army of Tumblr fans.

Social media as writers use it:

Samantha Priestley @SamPriestley

Writer and novelist Samantha Priestley finds that Tumblr works well in her social media mix - but that doesn't mean she posts the same thing everywhere: "I mainly use Facebook, Twitter and Tumblr. I also have pages on Pinterest and Instagram, but I use those less at the moment. I use them all differently. There might sometimes be an overlap in content and I post the same photos to all of the different sites, but readers know instantly if you are just pasting the same content into each of your social media sites. Interactions on each social media are different so you have to keep that in mind when you are posting to them. What works on Tumblr doesn't work on Twitter and so on. Tumblr is particularly good for blog posts and photos which are too long for Facebook and Twitter. I don't use any apps or tools to manage my social media. I update each one personally and do my best to keep up with it all!"

Sam's found that the main benefit to her has been much wider exposure of her work: "There's no better way to reach this many people. I have also made friends and work connections through social media. The most surprising thing I think I've gained though is support. Writing is a lonely business and social media allows you to connect with other people who are doing what you do and who can offer support and help when you need it."

Sam's advice to newbies? Be patient "It takes a while to build up connections through social media. Don't spam people with links and generic messages, nobody likes that. Present yourself as a person rather than as a business, it's less intimidating and more appealing to other users. Answer messages and interact as much as you can. It's no good setting yourself up a page on social media and waiting for people to come to you, you have to find connections and talk to people."

How Tumblr works

- **The Dashboard** - Your dashboard is where you'll spend most of your time. Every time you look at a Tumblr site, you'll automatically be invited to follow it, and as with all social media networks, you start by following plenty of people before you can reasonably expect anyone to follow you. Here you can see a live feed of whoever you're following and you can comment, reblog, and like posts from other blogs. The dashboard will let you write text posts, upload images, video, quotes or links via a button displayed at the top

- **Queue** - To manage your time, you can set up a schedule to delay publishing posts you create.

Your posts can be spread over several hours or even days

- **Tags** - Each time you create a post, you can help your readers find posts about certain topics by adding tags - this is very similar to the hashtag # system we saw on Twitter, except the tag has its own box and if you tag elsewhere it doesn't count.

- **HTML editing** - Fancy stuff! Tumblr allows you to edit your blog's theme HTML coding to change its appearance. You can also use a custom domain name for your blog, much as you might do for your main website. If your Tumblr IS your main website then this makes sense.

Above all, Tumblr is a community rather than a chance for you to broadcast your thoughts to the world. You can ask readers to ask you questions and open up plenty of dialogue around your book. Always, always respond to anyone who makes contact with you or sends you a question. Whilst the actual creation of content for Tumblr doesn't take long, the interaction and community aspect of it can do. But if you want engaged readers who will fly the flag for you, this is how to attract them. Tumblr users have a very high bullshit detection rate, so if you're there primarily to sell and promote Brand You then this will be a total turn off. Be genuine, be generous, be humble, be helpful and Tumblr will embrace you.

YouTube
YouTube is another Google-owned product, so if you have a Gmail account you will already have a YouTube account and channel to go with the G+ profile they gave you, whether you want them or not.

YouTube videos show up higher in search engines than other forms of content, so it's worthwhile including a few videos on your blog or Tumblr. You can also use your YouTube channel to curate material created elsewhere - perhaps you've been on TV, given a talk or participated in a Google Hangout. This is a way to share that material with the many people who weren't there to see it live. You could also film stuff on your phone or laptop and then upload it directly to YouTube. From there you can use the embed code to plant the video on your website or blog. Just remember to hold your phone sideways, otherwise you will get a very squeezed and narrow picture.

Many writers get a little squirmy around YouTube because we are now tipping into the arena of the extrovert, and most of us writers, well, we're pretty introverted aren't we? Actually, I think if you can push yourself out of your comfort zone a bit then YouTube videos can be a good way to develop your public speaking skills. You can give a talk from the comfort of your own home, just you and your laptop's webcam, and then share it with many more people than might have come to see you speak in real life. And if you are giving a talk somewhere to real life people, always ask if it will be filmed or arrange to do it yourself. That way you only have to do the talk once but you will reap the benefits of it multiple times. Though the down side to this is that you can't keep rolling out the same old talk.

Social media as writers use it:

Paola Bassanese @paolaenergya
Author Paola Bassanese's credits include Confessions from the Massage Couch and Strictly Walk Slimmer. Paola uses a mix of social media platforms to connect with her readers, and finds that it's the more practical

YouTube videos that attract the most hits: "YouTube can be great for creating promos and trailers for books or profiles for authors. It's best to put yourself in the shoes of your readers - what would be interesting for them to watch? My most popular videos feature practical advice - what can you share with others that could be useful?

"I prefer using Twitter over other social media channels because it's more immediate. I also quite like Google+. I use Instagram to post a mix of pictures, from what I do/see on a day to day basis to the occasional book promotion. Pinterest can be very useful for writers as long as you mix promotional images with other images (for example, your favourite books, places of inspiration). I make sure I update my website regularly and when I have the time I read fellow independent authors' books and write a review.

"As a writer, social media has allowed me to connect with journalists, fellow authors, potential readers and experts to interview for my books. I managed to get some peer reviews ahead of publication through Twitter and have been canvassing to get more Amazon reviews for my books.

"I would say to choose one platform first - do some research to see where your readers/potential readers are and start networking with them (no sales pitches!). Show a genuine interest in them, ask them questions. The best social media profiles have only a bit of self-promotion, and share useful information - for example, if you are targeting potential readers and you write nonfiction, you can have links to relevant news and tutorials or create your own. Being good at conversation helps - find people who share the same passions as you and conversation will flow."

What to post on YouTube?

A vlog (video blog) doesn't have to be long - in fact shorter is better. Look at the success of Vine, with its looping six second clips. Film quality wise, it can be pretty rough and ready. If you're filming a video, be aware of the background behind you and remove any drying washing or distracting mess. Leave up any books that make you look erudite.

Once you've channelled your inner extrovert, you could ask someone you know to interview you about your work, or ask readers to send in questions for you to answer. Or just talk to the camera. Imagine yourself talking to one person only, and talk to them as you would a friend. Be as natural as possible and don't worry too much about stumbling over words. You're a human being, not a robot. John Green's videos are often very straightforward and not too fancy pants, yet his passion and sincerity connects with people. Watch other YouTubers' channels to pick up presentation tips (or how not to do it), but don't compare your videos to anyone else's.

Social media as writers use it:

Peter Jones @peterjonesauth

Peter Jones is the author of several popular self-help books on the subjects of happiness, love & losing weight and one chick-lit-rom-com novel. An enthusiastic user of social media, he can be found on Facebook, Instagram, Twitter, YouTube and blogs.

Peter started his YouTube channel as a way to squeeze more out of radio interviews: "I've found radio interviews on their own are pretty ineffectual. No one is listening. Or at least, no one is listening AND in a position to do anything about whatever it is you're promoting – they're either driving, or working, or on a rooftop somewhere. Regardless of how charismatic you are, once the interview's over – you're forgotten! And it doesn't matter how big the radio station is (I've been on BBC Radio Two and the World Service) or how long you're on air (I have a monthly self-help slot on a local radio station) - it's *still* ineffectual. BUT, put that interview on the web, where people can find it, listen to it, and get to your book within a click or two, and then that interview is definitely worth doing.

"I like YouTube because (once I've converted the audio into a video) it's easy to manage, and that video can be embedded into a blog post, or a Facebook post really really easily. And people like YouTube. They're familiar with that big red play button. They're more likely to click that than read what looks like a lot of words. Of all the posts on my blog, the audio posts are the most popular.

"All the stats I collect suggest that my social media activities are probably only responsible for 20% of my book sales. If that. What social media has given me is

1. A way to interact with my existing readers - which is both fun, and presumably increases the likelihood that they'll buy the next book, or recommend me to a friend.

2. Office banter – the life of a full time author is a lonely one. Twitter and Facebook take the place of work colleagues.

3. Networking – I've met some very useful people via social media. The author Keris Stainton was really helpful back when I was starting out. I found Alison my proof reader. I met and became great pals with Jamie Anderson (son of the late great Gerry Anderson). All have played a part in the production of the five books I've written so far. And the list goes on and on.

Peter's advice for new writers is to drop the promotional aspect, at least at first: "If you're unpublished forget about using social media to plug yourself – you're not at that stage yet. Use it as a networking platform to schmooze with other unpublished writers, and to make contacts.

"If you *are* published dismiss immediately the notion of creating a Facebook fan page for you the author. Only 1% of the people who 'like' that page will *see* your posts, and even less will interact with it or do anything useful (…unless you're willing to pay Facebook to 'boost' a post of course, but honestly, that doesn't make financial sense). Instead, use your Facebook profile as your author platform. What do you mean you want to keep some posts for friends and family only? Why?? What on earth are you saying to them that you can't tell the world? Stop that immediately.

Above all, published or unpublished, remember that it's SOCIAL media. Not SELLING media. So be social. Say something funny or interesting. Keep your promo activity to a minimum, and find new, interesting ways to plug stuff."

The dark side of the Tube

The down side of appearing on YouTube is that the commenters are often less than kind and much less than polite. Of course, most of them are lovely. But those aren't the ones who will irreparably damage your self-esteem. So if you do start receiving ordure from the commenting masses, you may want to turn off comments on your videos. But then the problem with doing this is that it takes away the conversational element which makes social media so social. All in all, comments are worth keeping as long as you brace yourself for the occasional invasion of the idiots.

There are few writers for whom a YouTube channel makes sense as a lead social media platform, but it definitely has its uses as an optional extra. The exception to this, as with Tumblr, is anyone who's wanting to reach the YouTube generation. If you want to speak to Young Adults, there's no more direct way to do so.

Also, don't try to be the next John Green. Just be the first you, it's easier.

And if you really can't face doing a piece to camera but want to explore the more visual side of social media, take a look at Pinterest and Instagram instead.

8. Pinterest and Instagram

Good for:
- Sharing pictures of lovely, lovely things
- Creativity and new ideas
- Connecting with new audiences

Not so good for:
- If you don't like taking pictures or don't have a smartphone, don't bother
- Direct sales or attracting work
- Possible time suck

In this chapter we're looking at:
- What Pinterest and Instagram are and the basics of how they work
- How they might be useful to you as a writer
- Ideas for how to use them to promote your work

Pinterest and Instagram are both photo sharing sites and apps, and both have the potential for incredible creativity. As writers, putting visuals to the forefront rattles our brains in a different way to words, and I think we all need that sometimes.

You are less likely to meet someone who'll hire you directly as a writer on Pinterest or Instagram, in the way that you might on Twitter or LinkedIn. However, you could well meet people who read your books, and gather inspiration which will make you a better writer. This will in turn make you more successful and likely to be published.

Social media as writers use it:

Rin Hamburgh @RinHamburgh

Freelance lifestyle journalist Rin Hamburgh finds that Instagram and Pinterest work well for her niche as part of her social media mix: "My main social media platform for work is Twitter, followed by Facebook, then Pinterest and then Instagram, though I also use all of them for pleasure too. I have a LinkedIn presence but rarely use it, other than to occasionally point people to for a more detailed CV than they might get on my website.

"I think that the point of social media is often less about getting work than about building a reputation and gathering ideas, both of which are vital to a writer. I am a lifestyle writer dealing with subjects such as crafts, home interiors, fashion, green living etc. So when I have boards on Pinterest that are full of well curated images, or my Instagram account is made up of pictures of my allotment or my latest knitting project, it all helps build a picture of me as an 'expert' (or at least someone who is involved) in these fields. I see Pinterest and Instagram as places where I can get a grassroots view of all sorts of trends, from the kinds of interiors people are attracted to, to the sorts of hobbies they're involved in, and this has often sparked ideas that I have pitched and had commissioned.

"I get the majority of my case studies and many of my expert quotes through Twitter and Facebook. I have also managed to make contact with elusive editors - one in particular is rubbish at emails but always responds to a tweet, while another is much more likely to send work my way if I comment on her Facebook photos. Finally, social media is an excellent source of ideas - as an example, when I noticed the increase of 'inspirational quote' pictures on Facebook and Pinterest a few years ago, I pitched an idea about how they had become the modern day self-help book, and the resulting feature was published in Psychologies magazine."

Rin advises social media newbies to stick to their passions: "Follow people you genuinely think are interesting, and share the kinds of information and imagery that you would want to see. Set goals, so you know what your aim is, and be sure to keep an eye on your analytics (Buffer is great for this, as is Hootsuite) and experiment to see what works. Most importantly, remember that social media is a place for conversation, not for you to endlessly shout out about how great you are or what it is you need. Don't forget how much you can gain from listening on social media, as well as talking."

What's the difference between Instagram and Pinterest?

All About Instagram
Though you can visit the Instagram site via your computer, you can't do much else there since it's an app that's mainly used via smartphones. With Instagram, the photos you're sharing are probably your own that you've either taken with your phone or uploaded via a camera. It's a very simple, free app to use since it's solely focused on taking and sharing photos. It's got over 300 million active users (more than Twitter), and you don't get

that big if your app is hard to use. You can also create and share videos of up to 15 seconds long.

This makes Instagram different and more personal and creative than a lot of other social media sites which encourage sharing of pre-existing material that somebody else made. You see something, you take a quick snap and you share it. It could be a beautiful flower, your child pulling a funny face or a stack of your books in a book shop. Technically it's hard to go wrong on Instagram. Sometimes photos don't upload because you're not connected to wifi but generally it's pretty foolproof.

Etiquette-wise, the rules are the same as other networks - don't spam people, be generous in supporting others and thank those that support you. And be sparing with the selfies.

The choice is yours whether you just share your image with your Instagram network or whether you also share it at the same time to Facebook, Twitter and other platforms. Personally, most of the time I only share to my Instagram people because a lot of them I also know on the other platforms too and I think it gets tedious for them to see the same thing more than once. I don't want to bombard people, even if I am quite pleased with that picture of a funny mushroom I just took. Also, I find that my Instagram tribe is distinct from my other tribes and it would be a mistake to use the same language to speak to all.

As a creative person, I like Instagram a lot. It's fun. Yes it takes more time to create your own photos as opposed to sharing somebody else's, but the rewards are so much greater. And it doesn't take *that* much time. The Instagram app contains many options for cropping and filtering your pictures so you can get them looking good. You definitely don't need to be a good photographer to be good at Instagram.

Because Instagram pics are personal and user-generated, they are a real insight into other people's lives. At least, the nice looking bits of other people's lives. It's a platform that's popular with both teens and women, so it's worth adding to your mix if you're looking to connect with them. Levels of interaction tend to be quite high, so expect some likes and a few comments whenever you post a pic and do the same for others in return.

Ever since Instagram as a company was acquired by Facebook, its pictures don't show up in Twitter feeds - tweeters have to click on an exterior link to see them. Therefore, even though you do have the option to share your Instagram pics via Twitter, more people will see them if you share them directly on Twitter (ie by going to the Twitter app and clicking on the Add a Photo option to upload your snap). It's a bit of a hassle, and combined with the overlapping networks previously mentioned, I don't usually bother and figure that anybody who needs to see it will. Just because you can share it far and wide doesn't mean you should.

Instagram is refreshingly non-commercial in nature, though many brands are starting to build a presence there. Links outside the main profile are not hyperlinked, so even if you leave a link as part of the caption to a picture people won't be able to click through it easily. Since it is so non-commercial, it's best to keep your levels of direct promotion to an absolute minimum. But that doesn't mean you can't do it at all.

Using Instagram to promote your writing
When my author's copies of How to Overcome Fear of Driving turned up, I was so excited that I took a picture of the box and

shared it on Instagram. Several people soon messaged me that they'd seen the title and were going to buy the book because it was something they needed. I didn't do it with promotion in mind, I was just overjoyed that it had finally been published. Sometimes your best promotion can come from when you're trying least hard to do it.

I've also shared Instagram pictures of magazines I've had something published in - angled so the viewer can see what it is but if they want to read the feature then they'd have to go and buy the magazine. I might also tag the publication using the @ symbol, and most of the time when they see that, the magazine will retweet it. This is one of the few instances in which I would recommend sharing your instagrams on Twitter, since publications are more likely to have a presence on Twitter than they are on Instagram.

Promotion-wise, this works on a couple of different levels - it tells your network what you're up to; advertises the magazine and shows them that you've got a network that you're prepared to promote them to. Publications like stuff like that - as I mentioned right at the start of the book, editors like writers who are connected; they've got a bit of a buzz about them.

What to share on Instagram?
If you're going somewhere interesting in the course of your writing, then Instagram is a great way to share that with people, like a virtual postcard from your travels. Perhaps you're going on a book tour or researching a story. Keep your eye open for something cool or fun or interesting to photograph. Even in your day to day life, once you start looking it's not hard to find a few photo opportunities.

Share anything you like that catches your eye. Probably the most popular pictures I share on Instagram are cakes I've made. Everybody likes a good cake pic, almost as much as they like a good cake.

Try to resist the urge to share too many selfies. Think about what your network is looking for. It's probably not your face from every angle. Let them view cake instead. The exception to this might be if you are a beauty writer, are engaging with a younger audience or if you genuinely do have a face that's wondrous from every angle.

Posting to Instagram is generally done less often than posting to Facebook and much less often than tweeting. It doesn't have to be every day. A few nice photos a few times a week is plenty - never feel you have to Insta just for the sake of it.

As with all social networks, take time to connect with other people - follow back people who follow you, and use the little heart symbol to indicate that you like a photo. And be generous with your likes. Whilst you might not do much direct promotion of your writing, you will be promoting you as a person, and this will have a direct effect on other people's willingness to check out your wares.

Tagging on Instagram

Tagging is the social media equivalent of tapping someone on the shoulder to get their attention. Just like on Twitter, add the @ symbol in front of someone's username to tag them, and they will get a notification on their phone that you did so. People tag each other to draw their attention to something, or to bring them into a conversation. More commonly it's used to nominate people to take part in memes (the online equivalent of a chain letter).

One very common meme on Instagram is #widn which stands for What I'm Doing Now. The idea if someone tags you for this is that you're meant to take and share a photo of what you're doing right at that instant, although what most people do is to wait until they are doing something more photogenic. Then when you share your photo, you tag a few people using #widn and they pick up the baton and so the meme moves on.

If all of that seems wildly complicated, don't panic! I was on Instagram for a couple of years before I worked out what the tagging business was all about. Don't bother tagging anybody at first, and when somebody tags you you'll know what to do.

All about Pinterest
In contrast to Instagram, which is more focused on pictures you personally create, Pinterest consists of collections of other people's photos that have taken your fancy online which you want to collect - essentially it's a virtual pinboard. It's your teenage bedroom wall with less Blu tack and more pixels, or, as its founders would have it "a visual discovery tool". You can use it to share images you create, but it's generally used more by collectors than creators.

Some websites block their copyrighted content from being shared on Pinterest. In general, if a site includes social media sharing buttons including Pinterest on its features and posts, then you're OK to share it on Pinterest. When you pin, you're agreeing that you have permission to share this image. Of course in practice a lot of people ignore that, but as writers I think we need to care about copyright and not take other people's stuff just because we found in on the internet.

Each image pinned links back to the original web source it came from, so it can be a source of traffic for your blog if you or somebody else pin images from there. Or you can use it to gather a group of online resources you want to save or sites you want to refer back to.

At the time of writing, Pinterest has around 70 million users, with more than 80% of those being women. People use it to plan their interior decor, plan holidays or diy projects or just to display collections of images they like. Simply follow the instructions to pin an image to one of your boards. You can even download a tool so that you can easily pin any image you want to - all of this is explained on the Pinterest site.

Pinterest is increasingly being used in education, with teachers creating boards to help plan lessons, and students using boards to gather resources for study. So if you do any lecturing or teaching, it may prove useful to you.

As with Instagram, you can follow other people's streams (or boards in the case of Pinterest) quite easily. Unless someone has marked their account as private (and most people don't - if you wanted to be truly private you wouldn't be on there in the first place), then you can follow them and they can follow you.

Your collections of pinned pictures on Pinterest is called a board, and you can create as many boards as you want. Followers might follow individual boards, or they might follow all your boards. If you have a board that you don't want people to follow then you can mark it as a Secret Board and it will only be seen by you.

Pinterest is more commercial in nature than Instagram since many people use it to collect pictures of stuff they intend to buy, and this has meant that many brands and companies are all over it like truffle pigs in the forest. Therefore you can get away with being slightly more commercial than you would on Instagram and plug your own books and blogs. But still try to keep it to no more than 20% sharing your stuff versus 80% sharing other people's.

Promoting your writing on Pinterest

As well as using Pinterest to generally establish yourself as A Good Egg and therefore worth hiring, you can also use it to directly promote your books and other published works. Create a board of your favourite books, and put your own book cover in there as the main cover image.

I have a board on Pinterest entitled Books I Love. It's got lots of book covers of books that have taken my interest, or which I've read and enjoyed. And yes, my own books are on there too, but I figure that's OK because I love them too. I wouldn't have spent all that time writing them if I didn't. But I have lots of covers and pictures in there of books that I didn't write. Anyone who follows my boards can see that too. I also have a pinboard for My Published Writing.

As previously mentioned, pictures that you pin on Pinterest will be attached to an original URL, so if you've got decent, original pics on your blog posts, Pinterest can be a way to bring them to another audience. Pinterest traffic tends to be ongoing, as the ripples spread slowly, in contrast to the quick burst of hits you might get when you share something on Twitter. Sometimes I will create a picture-heavy blog post precisely with Pinterest in mind. I'm doing that to bring readers to my blog in a steady, ongoing stream.

As with all social networks, community is key on Pinterest. Broaden your network and reach by pinning from a variety of sites, not just your own. You'll miss out a lot if all you ever attempt to do is promote yourself.

Group boards on Pinterest

You'll reach the biggest audiences on Pinterest if you pin to group boards, since lots of people are already there and sharing stuff and potentially looking at your pins and boards. A group board is simply that - a type of pin board that lots of people can pin to, like a noticeboard in your town square.

Many blogging networks will have group Pinterest boards which their members can join - I currently belong to two of those, and the rules are that you can't upload more than two pins a week, to stop people spamming the boards.

When you find a group board that you're interested in joining, ask the board owner if they'll let you in. If there's a group you're already in, find out if they have a group Pinterest board (most blogging and some community or study groups do) and ask to join. If there isn't one, offer to set one up, even if you're not sure how to. Great way to learn!

When you're looking at other people's pins or boards, you can click to show that you like someone else's image and then republish it to your own network. Repinning is very common and even encouraged on Pinterest, because it's how stuff spreads. It's less common on Instagram because, in the most part, those are people's own personal images.

Pinterest and Instagram are types of social media which people mainly use just for the fun of it, and I think it's precisely because these networks aren't overrun with people selling stuff that makes them so popular. Use them for fun and creativity first and with promotion very far behind that and you will get out more than you put in, in lots of ways.

Whilst you may connect with a new network on Pinterest, social media people do tend to spread themselves about, so you may find that the active people in your other social networks crop up here as well, particularly bloggers. Bloggers love a good Pinterest board. Though it may take you to a new audience, what Pinterest will also do is deepen your connections with the people you already know.

Getting started on Pinterest

When you register for a Pinterest account, it suggests a number of boards you might like to fill, but feel free to ignore these and create your own. Look for the Find Friends tab (under your name when you're logged in), but don't send out an invitation to everyone in your address book.

Use the search bar to look for boards on topics you're interested in. As with all social media, come with a generous heart and give many times before you take. It doesn't have to be time consuming to give - pin a picture, re-pin somebody else's, like a picture by clicking on the heart in the corner, follow somebody else's boards.

You'll find pinning a heck of a lot easier if you're using Google Chrome and install the Pin It app. This makes a Pin It button appear on any image, on any web page you're looking at, so all you have to do is click to pin.

You can also automatically set it up so Facebook and/or Twitter gets notified when you pin something, and the people in your network can see it. If you were a jewelry maker filling your boards with gorgeous pieces then there might be a point to this, but otherwise I think it's best avoided.

It's clear that whilst Pinterest and Instagram are both fun to use, neither of them are likely to act as a direct sales vehicle. It's more likely that you will enjoy them as experiences in themselves and maybe expand your network and enrich your relationships from other networks. So maybe you will follow people's boards and then talk to them on Twitter or Facebook and then maybe they will buy your books or hire you to write for them. In that sense it's very much a secondary network.

Out of the two, I much prefer Instagram, but that's a personal preference and yours may be different. I like being creative by taking pictures on my phone and sharing them more than I like collecting pictures and rearranging them on a board. My Instagram feed hardly ever relates to my writing, though the profile clearly states that I'm a writer.

Both Instagram and Pinterest are extremely easy to use, so if you have a play with them it's hard to go wrong. Stick with the one that engages you most, and if neither do then it just means you've got more time for Twitter. Or indeed writing...

We're almost at the end of our leap along the social media platforms, but before we go it's time to stop off at one of the most well-established versions of them all - forums, and Goodreads.

9. Goodreads and other specialist forums

Good for:
- Authors connecting directly with readers
- Journalists researching and looking for case studies
- Networking with other writers and learning from each other

Not so good for:
- Keeping you focused on your work
- Anonymous forums often bring out the worst in people

In this chapter we're looking at:
- Best practice in using forums
- How you can use forums to support your work
- What Goodreads is and how authors can best navigate it
- Some examples of forums you might find useful

How do forums differ from the other social media platforms we've looked at?
A forum is a club or group of people united by a shared interest or profession. It could include a few dozen people, or millions. Forums are a great way to connect with people around the globe who share the same enthusiasms you do - whether it's politics or beauty or a really weird breed of dog.

For authors and journalists with a specific niche, think about where your target audience might be, and seek out those forums. So for my book about fear of driving, I'm looking for forums on that topic, but also forums that deal with anxiety, and forums for therapists who might want to know about my book so they can recommend it to their clients.

A lurker is someone who follows the forum but doesn't post, and there will always be many more lurkers than active posters. Studies estimate that anywhere from 50% to 90% of any online community may be made up of non-participating lurkers. So whatever you post on a forum, including the ad for your website in your signature, will be seen by substantially more people than it may appear at first glance.

Many forums have their own language and acronyms, and if it's not a forum for writers then language does not have to be aiming for a Pulitzer Prize. But if you are there as a writer, under your writing name, then text speak, misspellings and errant apostrophes will not do. That's not how to advertise your wares.

It costs money to set up a forum so there will often be an official sponsor and a commercial intent. The exceptions to this are Facebook groups, which anybody can set up for free provided they don't mind operating under Facebook's umbrella.

As a writer forums can be great places for research and to connect with people you would never meet in day to day life, or they can be fun places to get advice and discuss your interests. And there are some excellent groups specifically for writers too.

Online forums have been around for decades, well before the other social media platforms we've been looking at in this book. They were social media before it was even called that. As such you will find people on forums that you won't necessarily find on Twitter or Google Plus. However, having been there a long time, some forumites can be initially intimidating to newer community members. Don't let them put you off. Without new, active members any community will decay.

Social media as writers use it:

Carole Edrich @C_E
Carole Edrich is a photographer and photojournalist specialising in dance. A long time user of online forums and groups, Carole's found that they can be great for accessing information, professional and personal relationships and attracting work: "A few of us formed a consortium and produced a tender to manage the Year 2000 changeover for Washington State and Seattle. I didn't initiate it but was approached for the same reason that everyone was selected: because out of all of the group (which must have numbered several hundred) we were the ones who had demonstrated in discussion that we knew our business best. We won the tender. The first time we met in real life was the night before we started the work, when we met in our hotel.

"Later I joined what was at the time a small revolutionary new community. Moblog was a group of people who shared their images, and through them their lives. My photography improved so much through this that I started taking photos of a sufficient quality to sell, until now I'm one of the foremost dance photographers in the UK and get most of my income through photography and photojournalism. Interaction with them is a constant source of inspiration for my journalism; especially for travel, technology and quirky personal stories. The same interaction also keeps me ahead of the curve on photography and new tech developments."

Best practice in using forums

Post under your own name
If you're using a forum or online group for professional reasons, always post under your own name even if some other posters remain anonymous. That's their choice, and it's fine if you wish to be nameless too but this will inevitably lead to you using the forum in a different way. Things can get nastier more quickly on an anonymous forum, which can be hugely entertaining but it can also suck up hours of your day.

Be upfront about your intentions
Don't pretend to be a regular punter if you have joined a forum with the intent of finding interviewees. Be honest and upfront about who you are and what your intentions are. Many forums have a media section for this purpose. Several also have copyright declarations stating that they own whatever people publish on their forum, so you can't just lift quotes from what people have posted.

Lurk a little but not too long
Wait a little before you start posting so you get the lie of the

land. Never join a forum and start posting straight away - this is the equivalent of arriving at a party and braying a monologue as soon as you enter the room. You need to get a feel for the place first. You need to learn to speak this forum's language. Who are the big noises? What's the etiquette? If people use acronyms, what do they mean?

But don't leave it too long as you might get too cosy in the shadows. If you are struggling with the etiquette then approach a moderator or community administrator for help.

Introduce yourself - say hello and join the group. In many forums your introductory post is the place where you get to be the most overtly promotional so this may be your biggest chance to promote your wares. Tell the group what you're bringing to the party and what you're hoping to gain, although maybe not as overtly as *I want you all to buy my books then never bother me again.*

Don't get intimidated by long term posters who act like they own the place

Every forum has at least one person who is probably fluffy and cuddly in real life but who mutates into a big scary bear online. They may not even know they're doing it. New users find forums with long term posters scary but ultimately they're just people like you.

The good side of people like this is that you can usually spot them a mile off, so you will probably notice them during your first ten minutes of membership and can then decide what approach you're going to take. Personally I avoid having arguments with people on the internet as much as possible because that way madness lies. There's always someone online who's getting it wrong and statistically at least some of the time that person will be you so it's best to take a chilled attitude. Also it is kind of rude to arrive anywhere and assume you know better than the people who've been there for years. This is why lurking a little at first is worth the wait.

Give before you take
If you bluster in asking for contacts without stopping to get to know anyone, it's unlikely to be well received. I see this a lot in journalism forums, where there are many posters you never ever see until they're after something. Don't assume that having less experience means that you have less to contribute. You may be less experienced work-wise than other forum members but you can still give opinions, help others or just liven the place up with your youthful joie de vivre. If you're a good egg you'll be welcome - there's not a forum twinkling on the internet that couldn't benefit from more good eggs.

This is also true for non-media forums dealing with sensitive or personal subjects. Tread carefully when you're entering those people's personal space, especially if you're hoping to persuade them to be case studies for you. I know several real life journalists who find amazing case studies via special interest forums, and they all say that it takes an investment of time to get those people to open up to them. This is why real life journalism may appear to pay well, but when you look into the time that goes into gathering the stories, it's well earned.

Include a bit of promotional blurb in your signature, if it's allowed
Many forums do not allow you to link out to your blog or website within your post, because they don't want people

leaving their site. However, a lot of the time it's OK to have some promo stuff in your forum signature, which is great because then people can see it every time you post.

Check the regulations before you do any promoting and look out for what other people do. For example, the Amazon user forum has a thread specifically for authors to introduce themselves and talk about their books, but if you tried to do that anywhere else the members would not be pleased at all.

User forums on Amazon

And while we're on the subject of Amazon, make sure you fill out your author page on there. Whilst the world's biggest bookseller does have user forums, and a few places where authors can plug their books, tread carefully with these and spend some time reading before you post anything.

The best place to promote your writing on Amazon, where you're actively encouraged to do so, is via your Amazon Author page. People do read that stuff, so fill yours out if you've got anything published on Amazon. For years I was getting hits to my blog from my Amazon author page without ever having filled anything in or adding any links.

You can claim your author page on the Amazon sites for the USA, UK, Germany, France and Japan. Tweak your biography as necessary depending on the audience. By the time you've written a book you may well have led an interesting life, so highlight the best bits. You don't need to put your full CV. Keep your blurb short, but mention anything that's relevant to the subject of your books. Include links to your social media platforms. This is a space for a free advert so make the most of it. You can also link your Twitter feed to it, and news of any forthcoming events.

Using media sections on forums

If you're looking for case studies, some forums have dedicated media request areas. Usually these are free, but occasionally sites will charge you to post a request. If you are thinking of paying for a media request, ask around amongst your fellow writers as to whether they have done the same and found it useful. No point in wasting money when there are lots of free options available.

Don't just put up your media request then leave - stick around a bit in case there are any questions about what you're after. Many forumites, especially in anonymous communities, will need warming up a bit before they agree to speak to the media. This obviously takes time, so it's not the best choice if you're on a short deadline, but if you're undertaking longer term research, such as for a book, then it can be time well spent.

Remember that nothing is private on the internet

If you're participating in a forum which is only open to registered members, or a secret Facebook group, anyone can still take a screenshot of what you've written and distribute it however they wish. So if you find yourself talking about someone online, don't say anything that you wouldn't say to their face. Even if it's a forum that you've been a member of for years and feels like a home from home - you never know who's lurking. If you think you are anonymous, somebody somewhere will probably be able to find out who you are.

Some forums you might enjoy:
Journobiz.com - Well-established journalism forum. Your next editor is either on here, or lurking
The No1 Freelance Ladies' Buddy Agency on Facebook - Good-natured virtual office banter and support
MediaWomenUK Yahoo group - Quieter than it used to be but still smooth like a snake
Goodreads - Of which more to come

Social media as writers use it:

Eve Menezes Cunningham @WellbeingEve

Freelance psychology, health and wellbeing journalist and holistic therapist Eve Menezes Cunningham is a big fan of Journobiz: "I absolutely love Journobiz and, more recently, the Freelance Ladies Buddy Agency on Facebook. I remember I used to see people post on Journobiz and I'd delete so many posts and feel so shy. But over time, I found more of my voice online and with my journalism. I cannot imagine being freelance without such resources.

"Also, I've made some wonderful friends through such online networking, one of whom recently pointed out, over dinner, that we were 'online friends' in such a creepy voice I almost fell off my chair laughing. I forget I don't actually know some of these people and yet, there's such generosity with encouragement, sharing strategies, contacts, potential opportunities, work, tech help and just general inspiration (one even sent me a cat cushion today because it made her think of the pics I post of my cat Rainbow). At a local Chamber of Commerce thing tonight, someone very

'networky' asked about networking and I felt stumped
(I don't do BNI or anything like that) and yet, while I
don't *think* of online as networking, it's a lifesaver."

Setting up your own online group or forum

I set up the online networking group MediawomenUK in
2005, when there was nothing at all online for women in media
to connect with one another. It's fairly dormant now as a lot of
those conversations have drifted over on to Facebook, though it
does spark into life from time to time and still has over 1100
members. Being a Yahoo group, people have to send and
receive emails to participate and these days we all get far too
much email, certainly much more than in 2005. That's
probably why email groups have largely had their day and
Facebook groups are on the rise.

It's easier than you might think to set up your own group or
forum and if you have an interest that might lend itself to
online discussion but hasn't already got an obvious outlet, why
not set one up? Being the one who starts the group is a great
way to boost your credibility amongst that group. You'll get to
be head cheese by default.

Finally, let's take a look at the world's biggest online book
forum. If you want to find a forum with readers and people
interested in buying books, hopefully your books, step this way.

Goodreads

I had never heard of Goodreads before I'd published a book,
but clearly I was well behind the curve because it has over 20
million users worldwide. No wonder Amazon bought it. Now
that I know it, I like it, but I'm a little bit scared of it too.

Essentially, Goodreads is an enormous online book club. You can keep track of all the books you've read, and the ones you'd like to read, on your own virtual bookshelf. If you're a bookworm searching for your tribe, here they are. If you're an author, you need to be here. If you'd like to be an author one day, you're welcome too.

You can give away promotional copies of your book, and the recipients will more than likely post a review on Goodreads too. People who enter your giveaway may also add your book to their To Be Read shelf, increasing its visibility across the site.

Again though, there is the potential for mucho time suck, especially if you join multiple groups - and there are lots and lots to choose from depending on what sort of reading or writing you're into. Make sure that you've filled out the biography section and have all your books listed, especially if you're published under more than one name.

As with other social media platforms, you have the option to connect on Goodreads with people you already know, if you authorise the site to look at your Facebook, Twitter or Gmail. Think carefully before doing this because nobody likes a spammy author. You will be unsurprised to hear that I don't think it's a good move.

If you've already got a book published, it's important to claim your author page on Goodreads because this then unlocks lots of other possibilities. You can start a blog directly on Goodreads or (probably a smarter use of your time) import a feed to your existing blog so that when you publish a post it shows up there as well.

I know I don't spend as much time as I could on Goodreads. If I was only writing books I probably would, but since I'm also a freelance journalist with ongoing deadlines then more immediate platforms such as Twitter and Facebook grab my attention more. I just popped on there when I was writing this and found somebody who says she's reading my fear of driving book right now. This thrills me immensely and I'm resisting the urge to ask her how she's getting on with it because, really, that would be kind of stalky wouldn't it?

How I use Goodreads is: every so often I will go in and add a list of more of the books I've been reading. I keep a list of them in ye olde Filofax. I know! Pen and paper! Don't tell my Twitter buddies.

By adding to your list of books, you're creating a virtual version of your bookshelf at home, and you know how nosy people can get about those. It's another way to present you the author, the brand (yeuch), to the world. What you've read speaks volumes about who you are and how you write.

Some Goodreads users will judge you if you have more friends than you have books listed. They will suspect (and to be fair, they might be right) that you're an author who's only there to hassle people to buy/read/review your books. So use it like it was designed to be used and load in plenty of great books you've read.

The Goodreads author groups are worth checking out, especially if you are self-published and doing all the marketing yourself. You can pick up a lot of good tips in there, particularly about how to present your books on Amazon. And given that Amazon now owns the site, if you want to sell a lot of books on there, a Goodreads presence isn't going to hurt.

Huge, well-respected authors have a presence there, as do authors just starting out. Like any big site it can be daunting at first but stick with it and you might grow to love life in the virtual book club.

As always, you do have to be careful about coming across as spammy, but Goodreads offers a number of options to promote your books:

- Add an ebook excerpt of your book. Just like the excerpts people can read from Amazon Kindle, you can upload a little piece of your book and Goodreads users can download it to read immediately.
- Add videos. This is great if you've done a talk or made a TV appearance that's been uploaded to YouTube, or you could make your own videos via Google Hangouts on G+ and help them reach a wider audience.
- Start a group. It's always easier to stand out in a networking group and get to know people if you're the one who started it in the first place. But don't just use the group to promote your own stuff - that soon gets tired.
- Create a book list. Books you like, books you'd recommend. Don't worry about trying to please everybody because that's impossible. Be honest about the books you think are good and those who agree with you will be drawn to you in time.
- Offer a giveaway of your book. As mentioned above. You can only give away physical copies of books for these giveaways (not Kindle versions).

- Add the Goodreads widget to your website or blog. Join up your online presence a little by showing off your list of Goodreads books on your website too. It's a fairly simple task of adding in a little bit of code. If you've got as far as launching your blog then you'll be able to do this easily.

- Advertising options. As with Facebook and Twitter, you can pay to promote on Goodreads. You set your own budget so it doesn't get out of control and can choose to target specific, relevant groups. If you are particularly time-squeezed then this may be worth a try.

If you find you really love Goodreads and want to hang around there more, once you have 50 books on your shelf you can apply to become a Goodreads librarian and help other users out. If you always wanted to be a librarian in real life, go for it. But to my mind this is starting to stray into the territory where time-wise social media could potentially take more than it gives.

Social media as writers use it:

Keris Stainton @Keris

Successful author Keris credits social media with "pretty much my entire career. In 2003, I started a blog to get into the habit of writing every day. I joined a writers' forum and made loads of friends and got fantastic feedback on my writing. More recently, my new agent and last two book deals came out of relationships I'd established on Twitter. Blogging and Twitter have always been my favourites. These days it's more Twitter than blogging. I've only just joined Instagram, but I'm loving that too. Facebook's useful for writing in that I will ask my friends questions about things I'm working on, but that's just for friends, it's not public.

"I mostly use Goodreads to keep track of my own reading and to spot new books I might like to read. I think 'best practice' for writers is not to read reviews of their own work on there. And if you do read a review (because it's so hard to resist), absolutely do not respond. Ever."

Keris' advice to newbies is to be your authentic self "Don't feel you have to create a brand or a persona, authenticity is the only way. Be friendly and interact with others - it's a conversation, not a broadcast. And don't constantly promote your writing or book. Obviously you can mention what you're up to - people following you will be interested in what you're doing - but constant promo is just irritating. Oh and absolutely don't use one of those auto-DM things."

All in all, online forums have a lot to give writers of every flavour.

So that's our tour of the current social media platforms - the only question remaining is which one are you going to start with?

Finally, check out the resources section for a handpicked collection of apps, websites and programs all designed to make your social media life a piece of cake. A piece of cake you can share on Instagram, naturally.

10. Tools of the Trade: Resources, Apps and Links

Whatever you want to do on social media, there will be an app or a tool to help. And if there isn't, perhaps you have stumbled across your next great invention.

New resources spring up every day, so this isn't intended to be an exhaustive list. These, I hope, are the best of the best. They're the resources, apps and sites I've used, or people I trust use, and recommend.

If there is something in particular you want to do on social media and it's not mentioned here, google for it because it probably exists. Or better still, ask your network on Twitter, Facebook, Google Plus or LinkedIn. Those people are good at that.

It's unlikely that you'll need all of these tools, so I would suggest reading this chapter with a notebook at hand to take a note of the ones you want to start using.

In alphabetical order we have:

ALLTOP
Alltop is a website offering a mix of the most popular headlines from around the world. The home page is very minimalist, so what you get is a list of links, which you can hover over to get a snippet of the content. You can also create an account and decide what sort of topics you want to see links to. It's great for suggestions of stuff to tweet about or link to on your G+ or

Facebook page. If you're struggling to come up with your own content to link to, you can curate some from here. It's also useful if you're running a social media account for a brand and want to find content on their topics of interest.

http://alltop.com/

AMAZON AFFILIATES

Being an affiliate for a company means that when someone buys something on your recommendation, you get a small cut (often around 5%). So if you link to any sort of products on your blog, especially your own books, it's worth signing up to Amazon's affiliates scheme.

Then if somebody clicks through your affiliate link and buys one of your books, you would not only earn your regular royalties, you'd also get a 5% affiliate fee. You're probably advertising your books already on your site, so why not? The individual amounts involved are tiny, but it all adds up with no extra effort from you. You also get 5% of anything that person buys after they've clicked through your link. It's important to be transparent with your readers if you're using affiliate links, so have a disclosure page on your blog which states that you do this.

Lots of companies offer affiliate schemes - I'm also signed up with other companies I've used as a customer and am happy to promote on my blog. I've earned several hundred pounds from these affiliate schemes in the last year - not a massive amount, but nice to have and not something I had to take any extra time or effort to obtain. It more than covers the cost of running the blog.

https://affiliate-program.amazon.co.uk/

https://affiliate-program.amazon.com/gp/associates/
promo/affiliate-programs.html

BIT.LY

This is a URL shortening tool that will let you track exactly
how many people clicked on a link. You can use it to compare
how the same link does over time and on different networks. So
you can see how many people clicked through from Twitter at
4pm versus those who did so when you sent the link at 3am
versus those who saw it on Facebook and clicked through from
there. It helps you work out which links resonate with people
the most and are therefore worth doing more of.

Most of us don't really need to know all that stuff, to that level
of detail, unless you are working as a social media manager and
need to report back to your client as to how effective their
campaigns are.

https://bitly.com/

BLOGLOVIN

I know! They forgot the G! Let us join our pedantic hands and
pray a pedant's prayer for the good folk at Bloglovin. This is a
site that enables you to both gather followers for your own
blog, and follow lots of other blogs. It means that you can read
a wide selection of blogs at once from one place, rather than
chasing lots of links around the internet. I like it enough to
forgive the erratic spelling.

When you start your blog, register it with Bloglovin and install the Bloglovin button on your site inviting people to follow you there. Each new post you publish will be added to your Bloglovin feed for your followers to see.

http://www.bloglovin.com

BUFFER

This is a scheduling tool, but it works in a different way to Hootsuite or Tweetdeck, of which more later. It's very useful for helping you find stuff to tweet about, and to tweet about the stuff you find. It's a good time saver and used by a lot of the people you might assume are on social media all the time. When you see a link that includes buff.ly then that was shared via Buffer.

To schedule, set the times you want regular updates to go out, and then set up a queue of updates, known as loading up your Buffer. On the free version you can have up to 10 updates ready to go, so even if you're only sending them twice a day it will last for a few days. Buffer will tell you when it thinks is the best time for your updates to publish, and you can either agree with this or set your own.

You can use Buffer to automate updates to a number of different social media networks, though as we discussed in the chapter on Facebook, you're always better off putting in updates directly on the Facebook site as more people will see them.

You can use it directly on the Buffer website, but it's probably more useful to download the Buffer plug in to your browser (don't panic, it's easier than it sounds). Once you've done this, then any time you find something online that you'd like to

share, all you have to do is click on the Buffer button. '
gives you the option to either share it straight away or in t
future. The good part is that you can do it all from the Buffei
app, so you don't have to fiddle around cutting and pasting and
logging in and out of various sites.

I mostly use Buffer for my KidsBlogClub site, especially for
feeding updates to the Google Plus page. While I want to keep
a presence on G+, I don't yet feel the need to go in there every
day. As I'm writing this book and building up my
@SocMed4Writers Twitter feed I'm using Buffer to provide
fresh tweets for that account every day. Within a couple of
minutes I can schedule tweets for the next week.

Buffer is also good for its content curation and the suggestions
it comes up with for stuff you might want to share. If you like
the look of those links, simply click the button and they're
scheduled.

If you are tight on time then Buffer is a great tool. You can
easily schedule a week's worth of social media posts by
spending 10-20 minutes on it once or twice a week. Just don't
get too hooked on the ease of scheduling. You still need to
show up as you once in a while to be truly social. For the
account that you want to keep ticking over easily, it's great. It's
just not quite enough to build up a totally engaged network by
itself. And for a beginner who's not sure what to tweet about,
it's a must.

https://bufferapp.com

DISQUS

A very widely used commenting system for blogs (also used by some newspapers and magazine sites). It makes it super easy to leave comments as once you're logged in, you stay logged in. It's very good at weeding out spam, so if you have it on your blog, you're much less likely to get spam comments showing up.

http://www.disqus.com

EVERNOTE

As an unrepentant stationery addict I refuse to be parted from ye olde notebook and pen. But my friends who prefer note-taking digitally can't get enough of Evernote, and over 10 million fellow users agree. From To Do lists to extensive research, you can store it all via Evernote. The advantage it has over offline methods is that you're not just restricted to the written word - you can take and store pictures; add web links; attach files and voice memos too. I think it would be particularly useful to a writer on the move. If you're travelling about doing interviews and conducting research then Evernote would be great. For somebody like me who barely leaves the house, well, I have a really nice pen.

https://evernote.com/

FEEDLY

Similar to Bloglovin, but not just restricted to blogs, Feedly is popular with users of mobile devices such as smartphones and tablets. Think of it as a personally curated news feed. If you tend to start your day jumping from link to link and checking out the same range of news sites, Feedly will bring all that stuff together and help you do it in a much more streamlined way. If you're inclined to procrastination (and as a writer you're probably hard-wired to it), this could help a lot. By bringing everything together it makes it easier for you to manage your daily reading. By not jumping from link to link you're less likely to fall into the rabbit hole of trying to read everything that's on the internet.

https://feedly.com/

FLICKR

A great source of images for your blog - search under Creative Commons for royalty-free images. Credit the photographer by linking back to them on Flickr. You can't use these images for anything commercial like a book cover, but a non-commercial blog post will be fine as long as it's marked Creative Commons and you credit the copyright owner.

https://www.flickr.com/

GOOGLE ALERTS

This service has been around since forever and still isn't totally accurate, but is definitely worth using. You can register for any alert terms you want and you'll get sent an email when new pages carrying those words are published online. Very useful if you're researching a particular topic or have an ongoing specialist niche that you need to keep on top of latest news for. Do register for alerts on your book title so you'll know if it gets mentioned online. Don't register for alerts on your own name, because that way paranoia lies.

https://www.google.co.uk/alerts

GOOGLE ANALYTICS

You may or may not need Google Analytics depending on how commercial you're planning to take your blog. If you're planning to host advertising, sponsored posts etc then you probably will need it because advertisers will be asking for the stats that GA provides. For professional bloggers it's a must. For everybody else, it's optional.

This tool provides detailed statistics of how many people have been visiting your site; what search engine searches took them there; how long they stayed and what else they clicked on. This can help you plan future content because you can see what's most popular with your readers.

All of the blogging platforms will provide a basic version of this information, but you get a lot more detail with GA so think about whether you actually need that information before you install it. If you're thinking that you might need it one day then install it today because it is not retroactive and will only count stats from the day it's installed.

Don't be downhearted if your stats are a lot lower than the stats in your blog's dashboard, because GA does not count bots (automated programs that crawl through your site and index it for search engines).

Some brands will ask to see GA information before they work with your blog so they can be sure that your stats are authentic, but that's very rare. I have GA installed on one of my blogs but rarely check it.

http://www.google.com/analytics/

HOOTSUITE

or possibly Tweetdeck because they do the same thing. These are free tools to help you manage multiple social media accounts. They're great because they let you do a lot of things from the same place, which saves a lot of time.

Use it to schedule posts, so you can be tweeting when you're asleep - very useful for reaching people in different time zones. Just make sure that you check back in soon to respond to any reaction to your post, and don't lose track of what you've scheduled in case you need to pull it. Even if you're not managing multiple accounts, the scheduling tool is worth using Hootsuite for. There's also an auto schedule button that chooses the best time to tweet for you.

You can use these tools from your phone but I prefer to use them on the laptop or PC so I can focus and avoid mistakes. There have been several instances of social media managers tweeting the wrong thing from the wrong account and you don't want that to be you.

And if you start picking up some social media work, you can use Hootsuite to run your client's Twitter alongside your own. You can also use these tools to manage Facebook and LinkedIn pages at the same time.

Hootsuite can give you analytics on how many people click through links that you send, which is useful for seeing what's popular with your network and when are the best times to post. You can also use them to focus in on what's most important to you, and thus avoid a lot of the flim flam that can make social media so confusing. Do this by setting up columns following particular hashtags, so you only see them and not every single tweet. If you have a particular specialism, or are researching a topic and need to see real time updates, this can be invaluable.

As well as topic, you can also organise what you see by people, so you can keep a separate column for the people whose tweets you don't want to miss. For example, if you write about celebrities or are stalking your exes, or if there are editors, publishers or magazines you're particularly trying to connect with, you could create a column just for these people.

I found Hootsuite to be a bit clunky at first, but worth persevering with. I sometimes use it to schedule tweets if I'm going to be away for a few days, or if there's a Twitter chat I want to contribute to but won't be around when it's taking place.

Once you've mastered the basics of Twitter then Hootsuite or Tweetdeck is a natural next step.

https://hootsuite.com/

INSTACOLLAGE

A lovely fun and free little app to help your images stand out on Instagram. Use it to create collages or add captions and frames. You wouldn't use it for every image but once in a while it comes in handy when you want to be more creative with your pictures.

https://itunes.apple.com/gb/app/instacollage-pro-best-hd-collage/id530957474?mt=8
https://play.google.com/store/apps/details?id=com.photos.instacollage&hl=en_GB

IFTTT

AKA If This Then That. This is another tool that automates stuff for you and saves you time. How it works is that it lets you set up an IFTTT recipe - IF I post THIS to Twitter, then THIS needs to go to Facebook THEN THAT to Google Plus. So you only need to post once and a whole bunch of stuff happens.

Extra timesavers offered by the tool include: changing your profile pics across multiple networks at once and sending daily texted reminders. Or you can set it so that every time you post a picture on Instagram, it also gets stored in your online filing system.

Personally I don't use this app because I don't usually want exactly the same content to go to a number of different networks and if I did I'd want to do it myself and tweak as appropriate. But it's a very widely used and praised so I think it's maybe more for the Evernote users amongst you, rather than those of us who only ever do our organising armed with a nice pen.

https://ifttt.com/

KLOUT

Klout is a social media monitoring tool. When you sign up for an account, you link up with all your social media networks and it will give you a score out of 100 depending on how influential it judges you to be. Apparently 60 or above is really, really good. I'm usually a 60-ish so I'm not sure how good that is, but when I dip below it I cry.

Why does Klout matter? Well, to most people it doesn't matter at all. But to some companies in particular it really, really matters. Some brands, when looking for writers and especially bloggers to hire or collaborate with, will favour those with a higher Klout score, or will specify that they are looking for people with a Klout score of 60+. So if you're an online writer or professional blogger, then having a high Klout score matters for you.

You can also use it if you're thinking of sending out copies of your latest book to blogs for review - in theory the bloggers with higher scores will have a more engaged network so hopefully their reviews should have more impact.

One tip I would give you with Klout is that you don't have to add in all the networks it asks you for, and in fact it's a good idea to only add in your best, most active networks. So if you have a YouTube channel but you hardly ever post to it, don't connect it to your Klout because it will drag your overall score down.

https://klout.com

LINKWITHIN

You know when you read a blog post, and at the bottom of the post there is a line of other posts with the tagline "If you liked this, you might also like..." Well, LinkWithin is what does that. Once you've installed the code you don't have to do anything else as it all happens automatically. And if installing the code sounds ominous, don't worry. I managed it on several sites, and I know nothing about coding. You won't be able to add it on to Wordpress.com sites, but other platforms will accept it.

Using this tool will make your blog look better and encourage your readers to hang around by giving them targeted options of more stories to read. It's called making a site 'sticky' and hopefully it will help to create more fans of your writing.

http://www.linkwithin.com

MAIL CHIMP

This is a free email newsletter tool, though as such it is not as current as other forms of social media. I mean, honestly, who really claps their hands and says "Oh goody! A newsletter" and reads it from top to toe when one lands in their in box? Not me and I bet not you either.

A newsletter will connect you with a different kind of audience than other social media does, so think about whether that's your audience and what the benefits might be. Mail Chimp is free to use and provides a number of widgets so you can add a newsletter sign up box to your website or blog. You could always add this in and see if many people sign up. If it looks like it's popular with your audience, then it might be worth taking the time to do.

And if people do sign up, cherish those people. They are interested in what you do and want to hear more. You can't buy that.

The Mail Chimp site contains a number of pre-made templates and many colour options to make your newsletter look nice. It can be a bit clunky at times to use, and you may struggle with this if design is not your natural forte. But this is often the price we pay for using free stuff. You want it easier, you'll have to pay for access or pay somebody else to do it for you.

Around 10 years ago I used to send a regular monthly email newsletter with specially written content. Then when I started the blog, the newsletter consisted of links back to that stuff. Then I cut it back to once a quarter, and now I don't even do that. I send sporadic updates and a Christmas greeting. I still have my mailing list on my Mail Chimp account, but because I don't use it often a lot of the addresses are now out of date and I get told off by Mail Chimp for not having a clean list. This is important because they will suspend your account if they suspect you're too spammy, and how they work this out is by how many of your newsletters bounce back.

Ultimately, given how so many of us get too much email these days, only add to the avalanche if it seems like a better way to reach your readers. Maybe your regular readers aren't on other social media platforms, or aren't the sort of people to feel overloaded with email. Or maybe you're a copywriter creating communications for an organisation that wants to run a newsletter. If you want to start an email newsletter, Mail Chimp is a good, free way to do it.

http://mailchimp.com/

MANAGEFLITTER

There are many tools to help you manage your Twitter network, and MangeFlitter is the best cleanup tool I've found. It will let you look at your Twitter followers and tell you who's not following you back, who's stopped tweeting, who might be a spammer and much more. You can then choose to unfollow up to 100 people at a time, easily and swiftly. If they aren't following you and don't seem to be tweeting any more then effectively they've left the room so there's not a lot of point in you staying connected.

If you feel overwhelmed by the number of people you're following on Twitter, or the people you're following aren't as interesting as you hoped they'd be, use ManageFlitter to do some pruning.

http://manageflitter.com/

NOVELRANK

I'm almost hesitant to recommend this because, authors, it has the potential to drive you crazy.

Novelrank tracks the movement of your books on Amazon, and tells you how many you've sold and when the last sale was. If your book's not listed then you can upload it and start tracking your sales.

Where this comes in very handy in association with social media is that if you do any sort of promotion, you can immediately see what effect that has on your sales. And if you have an unexpected spike or lull in sales, you can then investigate what's causing that too. Since your only other source of sales information may be a once a year statement from your publisher, this is very valuable to know when you're working out what sort of marketing works (and hence is worth doing more of), and what doesn't.

The crazy-making down side comes when you find yourself tracking book sales every day, or several times a day. And it can be quite disheartening if you've put a lot of effort into promotion but it doesn't produce any immediate results. All in all this is a useful tool, but proceed with caution.

http://www.novelrank.com

OTRANSCRIBE

Not strictly speaking a social media tool, but my writer compadres give this free transcription app the big thumbs up. Invaluable for anyone with interviews to transcribe, thus saving you time which you can then waft away on Twitter.

http://otranscribe.com

PICMONKEY

This simplified version of Photoshop is SUCH a useful site, and quite fun to play with too. You can build collages and edit existing photos; add text; crop and resize. It makes creating beautiful images for your blog, Pinterest, Facebook and the rest incredibly easy. You will need to resize images for your Twitter profile and Facebook header and this is probably the easiest way to do that. Occasionally it doesn't work too well, and when that happens I use a site called Fotor which does much the same thing.

http://www.picmonkey.com/

RAFFLECOPTER

Rafflecopter is a free tool to help you run contests and giveaways on your blog. It's one of those tools that looks like it should be complicated, but is actually very simple to use and a real time saver, as you can use it to set a number of different entry mechanisms at once. People often use giveaways to boost their website traffic and social media numbers, so entry options might include following you on Twitter or Instagram, circling your Google Plus page etc.

Rafflecopter will close the contest at the time you set, then you can use it to randomly pick a winner and show it on the widget. What it won't do is promote your contest for you, so you'll still have a bit of legwork to do there. It also doesn't check the authenticity of winners, so say if you pick a winner who says they entered by following you on Twitter, then you need to check that they actually did.

http://www.rafflecopter.com/

TRIBERR

Confession: I don't like Triberr. I mean, I've never used it, but I know enough to know that it is not my cup of tea. As the name suggests, Triberr consists of Tribes of people promoting each other's content. You can join multiple tribes. If you approve someone else's content, then you either take the lazy route and approve it without reading, or you take time to read it, thus negating the time you were supposed to be saving.

One thing it is good for is for building up close relationships with people in your tribe, as you become a mutually supportive group, but then you could've done that anyway, more easily elsewhere.

I'm not really selling this am I? Some people love it, so it's a bit like Marmite in that respect (I don't like Marmite either). At least now you can nod knowledgeably when it comes up in conversation.

http://triberr.com/

TWEETDECK
see HOOTSUITE

The social media management tool Tweetdeck is completely free, whereas Hootsuite has a free and paid for version. They're very similar, so it's just a matter of what you prefer.

And finally...

So now you've got the social media knowledge - what next?
Since a perceived lack of time is one of the major stumbling
blocks to getting more involved in social media, here are 15 five
minute (or less) social media actions you can take right now

1. Post a comment on three blog posts. I find Bloglovin
   very useful for this - I go to my dashboard of blogs
   I'm subscribed to and open up any links that appeal.

2. Share one of your old blog posts on Twitter

3. Find five editors on Twitter and follow them

4. Reply to three new people's tweets

5. Look at your most recent new followers on Twitter
   and follow back the ones who seem relevant

6. Pin an image to Pinterest

7. Add a couple of comments or likes on Facebook.
   Check out what the people you know are up to and
   respond.

8. Open a draft new post in your blog and just type
   without stopping for five minutes to see what comes
   out. It might be great, or it might be rubbish. Nobody
   will see it anyway if you don't hit the Publish button
   so why not try it - you might just hit gold.

9. Add a book to your Goodreads bookshelf

10. Comment on a thread in a group you belong to in
    one of your social media platforms. Just don't get
    sucked into spending an hour there.

11. Go back to one of your draft posts and read over it. It might be closer to publishable than you think.

12. Do an online search for your specialist writing niche. Restrict your search to the last week so you can what's brand new in your field - there may well be a number of articles in there for you.

13. Set up a Google Alert for a topic related to your writing niche

14. Set up a Google Alert for the titles of your previously published books

15. Schedule two tweets on Hootsuite

It matters more that you do this stuff regularly, than if you do a lot of it. Five minutes every day is better than four hours once a month. Show up; keep showing up; always look for ways to give value and you'll be your own best advert.

Acknowledgements

Many thanks to these wonderful writers for sharing with us how they use social media. Please now buy their books, follow them online and worship them as the highly-evolved beings they so clearly are

Jason Arnopp - Author and scriptwriter
www.jasonarnopp.com
http://www.amazon.co.uk/Jason-Arnopp/e/B0034OVY4U/

Paola Bassanese - Author
http://www.amazon.co.uk/Paola-Bassanese/e/B00HYUCT3U/
www.energya.co.uk

Patricia Carswell - Journalist, copywriter and award-winning blogger
www.patriciacarswell.co.uk
www.girlontheriver.com
www.fabulouswales.com

Dane Cobain - Writer and book blogger
www.socialbookshelves.com
www.danecobain.com

Jane Common Freelance journalist and author
http://www.amazon.co.uk/Jane-Common/e/B00J5K4ZHA/
www.phileasdogg.com

Emma Cossey - Freelance writer and freelance lifestyle coach
www.freelancelifestyle.co.uk

Carole Edrich - Publisher, Photographer and Writer specialising in dance, extreme and adventure sports and travel
www.webwandering.com
www.dancetog.com

Chloe Hall - Copywriter and Social Media Marketing Consultant
http://www.bumbleandbloommedia.co.uk/

Rin Hamburgh - Freelance lifestyle journalist
www.rin-hamburgh.co.uk

Ben Hatch - Author
http://www.amazon.co.uk/Ben-Hatch/e/B0034NT4U2

John Higgs - Author
http://www.amazon.co.uk/John-Higgs/e/B0086FBMYE/
www.johnhiggs.com

Peter Jones - Author
http://www.amazon.co.uk/Peter-Jones/e/B004RMHCQC/

Eve Menezes Cunningham - Freelance psychology, health and wellbeing journalist and holistic therapist.
www.evemenezescunningham.co.uk

Samantha Priestley - Creative Writer, Novelist and Playwright
http://www.amazon.co.uk/Samantha-Priestley/e/B0034OTQR2/
www.samanthapriestley.co.uk

Alexandra Robbins – Author
www.alexandrarobbins.com
https://www.facebook.com/AuthorAlexandraRobbins
http://www.amazon.co.uk/Alexandra-
Robbins/e/B001H6NY8Q/

Keris Stainton - YA Author
www.keris-stainton.com
http://www.amazon.co.uk/Keris-Stainton/e/B003HRY8WO/

Thanks
A special thank you to Lia for help with the Tumblr chapter
and to Isaac for keeping the seat warm

More from the author
You can find out about Joanne Mallon's other books here
http://www.amazon.co.uk/Joanne-Mallon/e/B00J26CETS/

and find out more about media career coaching with Joanne
here
http://joannemallon.com/

or just say hello on Twitter
http://www.twitter.com/joannemallon

Lightning Source UK Ltd.
Milton Keynes UK
UKOW04f2110250315

248538UK00004B/251/P